KOUZES
POSNER

LEADERSHIP
PRACTICES
INVENTORY
(LPI)
ACTION CARDS

FACILITATOR'S GUIDE

JAMES M. KOUZES AND BARRY Z. POSNER
WITH JO BELL AND RENEE HARNESS

Package ISBN: 978-0-470-40447-8

Acquiring Editor: Marisa Kelley
Development Editor: Leslie Stephen
Editor: Rebecca Taff
Composition: MPS
Printed in the United States of America

Director of Development: Kathleen Dolan Davies
Production Editor: Dawn Kilgore
Manufacturing Supervisor: Becky Morgan
Design: Riezeboz Holzbaur Group

Printing 10 9 8 7 6 5 4 3 2 1

CONTENTS

Contents

WEBSITE TABLE OF CONTENTS

Our readers are invited to download customizable materials from this book. The following materials are available FREE with the purchase of this book at: www.leadershipchallenge.com/go/lpiactioncards

The following username and password are required for accessing these materials:

Username: facilitator
Password: action

Leadership Behaviors Board Game (Activity 1) supplies
    -Game Board (print on legal size paper)
    -Leadership Opportunity Cards
    -Game Pieces

ABOUT THE AUTHORS

Jim Kouzes and **Barry Posner** are coauthors of the award-winning and best-selling book, *The Leadership Challenge*. This book was selected as one of the Top 10 books on leadership of all time (according to *The 100 Best Business Books of All Time*), won the James A. Hamilton Hospital Administrators' Book-of-the-Year Award and the Critics' Choice Award from the nation's book review editors, was a *BusinessWeek* best-seller, and has sold over 1.8 million copies in more than twenty languages. Jim and Barry have coauthored more than a dozen other leadership books, including *A Leader's Legacy*—selected by *Soundview Executive Book Summaries* as one of the top thirty books of the year—*Credibility: How Leaders Gain It and Lose It, Why People Demand It*—chosen by *Industry Week* as one of its year's five best management books—*Encouraging the Heart, The Student Leadership Challenge,* and *The Academic Administrator's Guide to Exemplary Leadership.* They also developed the highly acclaimed *Leadership Practices Inventory* (LPI), a 360-degree questionnaire for assessing leadership behavior, which is one of the most widely used leadership assessment instruments in the world. More than 400 doctoral dissertations and academic research projects have been based on The Five Practices of Exemplary Leadership model.

Among the honors and awards that Jim and Barry have received are the American Society for Training and Development's (ASTD) highest award for their Distinguished Contribution to Workplace Learning and Performance; Management/Leadership Educators of the Year by the International Management Council (his honor puts them in the company of Ken Blanchard, Stephen Covey, Peter Drucker, Edward Deming, Frances Hesselbein, Lee Iacocca,

Rosabeth Moss Kanter, Norman Vincent Peale, and Tom Peters, who are all past recipients of the award); and named among the Top 50 Leadership Coaches in the nation (according to *Coaching for Leadership*).

Jim and Barry are frequent conference speakers, and each has conducted leadership development programs for hundreds of organizations, including Apple, Applied Materials, ARCO, AT&T, Australia Post, Bank of America, Bose, Charles Schwab, Cisco Systems, Community Leadership Association, Conference Board of Canada, Consumers Energy, Dell Computer, Deloitte Touche, Dorothy Wylie Nursing Leadership Institute, Egon Zehnder International, Federal Express, Gymboree, Hewlett-Packard, IBM, Jobs DR-Singapore, Johnson & Johnson, Kaiser Foundation Health Plans and Hospitals, L. L. Bean, Lawrence Livermore National Labs, Lucile Packard Children's Hospital, Merck, Mervyn's, Motorola, NetApp, Northrop Grumman, Roche Bioscience, Siemens, Standard Aero, Sun Microsystems, 3M, Toyota, the U.S. Postal Service, United Way, USAA, Verizon, VISA, and The Walt Disney Company.

Jo Bell and Renee Harness are managing partners at Third Eye Leadership, whose mission is to inspire organizational strength with courage and vision. They are experts in strengthening the organizational bottom line through evidence-based leadership experiences, such as The Leadership Challenge® Workshop. They are contributors to the second, third, and fourth editions of *The Leadership Challenge*, master facilitators of The Leadership Challenge® Workshop, and executive coaches utilizing the *Leadership Practices Inventory*.

Jo Bell. The seed of Jo's passion for leadership sprouted in a serendipitous introduction to Jim Kouzes in 1987 at a medical symposium; shortly afterward Jo began her leadership mentorship with him. Jo has been a master facilitator since 1998. Jo's earlier career in healthcare, which spanned seventeen years as a hematologist and director of clinical laboratories, gave Jo a strong foundation as a leader and a manager in understanding human behavior, motivations, and the impact on the core business. Jo is known for developing lasting customer partnerships through her genuine passion for leadership and her astute attention to the strategic alignment of the leadership development implementation. Jo has a bachelor's degree in clinical laboratory medicine, a master's degree in organization development, and a doctorate in hematology.

A Personal Message from Jo: *"I envision myself as an architect in designing an environment that stewards learning and leadership— one that refreshes and challenges. I consider myself a "Scout 4 What If!"… a life-long learner with a robust inquisitive nature. I believe the greatness for leadership lies within every individual—sometimes fossilized from insecurity, unawareness or the belief that it's reserved for only a few great men, a few great women, or the higher levels within an organization. It is my personal commitment to encourage others to stretch—to learn—to breathe life into—to seize the opportunity to lead. It is my charter to help others embrace leadership as an identifiable set of skills and practices available to all of us."*

Renee Harness. Renee has a discerning eye for creating a climate that appeals to the needs of leaders as learners and becomes a catalyst for open minds. Renee has been a facilitator of The Leadership Challenge since 1999, and a Master Facilitator since 2006. She has led organization development, training, and effectiveness initiatives in corporations and academia for more than sixteen years. Her roles in companies such as Charles Schwab & Co., Inc., and Roche Diagnostics, as well as several Indiana state universities, have focused on engaging the leader within people at all levels to create a climate of leadership and results through people. Her experience includes large-scale implementation of leadership programs at the executive, first-line manager, and employee levels. Renee holds a master of science degree in sociology.

A Personal Message from Renee: *"Leadership is not only a science, it is an art. And just as in fine art, there is more below the surface of our leadership than meets the eye. What sparks my passion about The Leadership Challenge is that I am not only helping leaders find the art of their own leadership, but that this has a positive impact on the lives of the people around these leaders. My commitment is to help leaders fully engage, develop, and excite the people they work with, creating an environment in which leaders get results through the passionate involvement of their people."*

INTRODUCTION

"The instrument of leadership is the self, and mastery of the art of leadership comes from the mastery of the self."
—Jim Kouzes and Barry Posner

Throughout their international best-selling book, *The Leadership Challenge*, Jim Kouzes and Barry Posner tell stories of ordinary people who have mobilized others to get extraordinary things done in virtually every arena of organized activity. They talk about men and women, young and old, from a variety of organizations—small and large, public and private, manufacturing and services, high-tech and low-tech. These leaders are not famous people or mega-stars. They're people who might live next door or work in the next cubicle. Kouzes and Posner focus on leaders like this because they firmly believe that leadership is not about position, but about relationships, credibility, and what people *do*.

"Ordinary" individuals can mobilize others to get extraordinary things done in organizations by practicing The Five Practices of Exemplary Leadership®, the leadership model Kouzes and Posner developed from a research project begun more than twenty-five years ago. To answer the question, "What is it that people actually *do* to get extraordinary things done in organizations?" Kouzes and Posner collected thousands of stories in which people described what they did when they were at their "personal best" in leading others. The personal bests were experiences in which their study respondents, in their own estimation, set their individual leadership standards of excellence.

THE FIVE PRACTICES OF EXEMPLARY LEADERSHIP®

From their analysis of thousands of personal-best leadership experiences, Kouzes and Posner found that, despite differences in people's individual stories, all the experiences followed remarkably similar patterns of action in a wide range of settings. As they looked deeper into the dynamic process of leadership, through case analyses and survey questionnaires, they uncovered five practices common to the respondents' personal-best leadership experiences.

When getting extraordinary things done in organizations, leaders engage in these Five Practices of Exemplary Leadership®:

- Model the Way
- Inspire a Shared Vision
- Challenge the Process
- Enable Others to Act
- Encourage the Heart

Over time and across continents, these five practices have endured as a model for how leaders mobilize others to transform values into actions, visions into realities, obstacles into innovations, separateness into solidarity, and risks into rewards. Even though the context might have changed since Kouzes and Posner began their research, the conclusion has remained the same: leadership is a set of skills and abilities that can be learned by almost anyone who has the desire and commitment to improve.

Embedded in The Five Practices of Exemplary Leadership® are behaviors that serve as the basis for learning to lead. Kouzes and Posner call these The Ten Commitments of Leadership (see Table 1).

TABLE 1. The Five Practices and Ten
Commitments of Exemplary Leadership

Model the Way

1. Clarify values by finding your voice and affirming shared ideals.
2. Set the example by aligning actions and shared values.

Inspire a Shared Vision

3. Envision the future by imagining exciting and ennobling possibilities.
4. Enlist others in a common vision by appealing to shared aspirations.

Challenge the Process

5. Search for opportunities by seizing the initiative and by looking outward for innovative ways to improve.
6. Experiment and take risks by constantly generating small wins and learning from experience.

Enable Others to Act

7. Foster collaboration by building trust and facilitating relationships.
8. Strengthen others by increasing self-determination and developing competence.

Encourage the Heart

9. Recognize contributions by showing appreciation for individual excellence.
10. Celebrate the values and victories by creating a spirit of community.

The *Leadership Practices Inventory* further translates The Five Practices into behavioral statements so that people can assess their skills and use this feedback to improve their leadership abilities.

THE LEADERSHIP PRACTICES INVENTORY (LPI)

The LPI is a 360-degree assessment instrument developed by Kouzes and Posner for two purposes: to test their initial findings that The Five Practices model is a valid view of the world of leadership, and to provide a tool that helps leaders assess the extent to which they actually use those practices so that they can make plans for improvement.

The LPI provides both self-assessment information and the perceptions of five to ten observers of a leader's leadership behaviors; it does not evaluate IQ, leadership style, management skill, or personality. The feedback provided is the foundation of improvement, and the first step in improving leadership practices.

To complete the LPI, individual leaders and their observers use a 10-point scale ranging from "almost never" (1) to "almost always" (10) to indicate how frequently they engage in thirty leadership behaviors, six behaviors for each of The Five Practices of Exemplary Leadership®. The ranking on one practice does not affect the ranking on any of the others.

The research data from hundreds of thousands of people consistently show that leaders who more frequently engage in the behaviors measured by the LPI—in other words, The Five Practices—are more likely to be identified as effective leaders. That's a key objective for the activities in this guide: For leaders to learn what The Five Practices of Exemplary Leadership® entail and develop their ability to comfortably engage in them more frequently than they are doing today.

The thirty leadership behaviors are listed in Table 2 according to the practice that they define.

TABLE 2. The Thirty LPI Behaviors Related
to the Five Practices

The Five Practices of Exemplary Leadership	The Thirty Leadership Behaviors of the Leadership Practices Inventory (LPI)
Model the Way	1. Sets a personal example of what he/she expects of others
	6. Makes certain that people adhere to agreed-on standards
	11. Follows through on promises and commitments
	16. Asks for feedback for how his/her actions affect people's performance
	21. Builds consensus around organization's values
	26. Is clear about his/her philosophy of leadership
Inspire a Shared Vision	2. Talks about future trends influencing our work
	7. Describes a compelling image of the future
	12. Appeals to others to share dream of the future
	17. Shows others how their interests can be realized
	22. Paints "big picture" of group aspirations
	27. Speaks with conviction about the meaning of work
Challenge the Process	3. Seeks challenging opportunities to test skills
	8. Challenges people to try new approaches

(Continued)

TABLE 2. The Thirty LPI Behaviors Related
to the Five Practices (*Continued*)

The Five Practices of Exemplary Leadership	The Thirty Leadership Behaviors of the Leadership Practices Inventory (LPI)
	13. Searches outside organization for innovative ways to improve
	18. Asks "What can we learn?"
	23. Makes certain that goals, plans, and milestones are set
	28. Experiments and takes risks
Enable Others to Act	4. Develops cooperative relationships
	9. Actively listens to diverse points of view
	14. Treats people with dignity and respect
	19. Supports decisions other people make
	24. Gives people choice about how to do their work
	29. Ensures that people grow in their jobs
Encourage the Heart	5. Praises people for a job well done
	10. Expresses confidence in people's abilities
	15. Creatively rewards people for their contributions
	20. Recognizes people for commitment to shared values
	25. Finds ways to celebrate accomplishments
	30. Gives team members appreciation and support

THE LEADERSHIP PRACTICES INVENTORY ACTION CARDS

Kouzes and Posner's research has shown that leadership is an identifiable set of skills and abilities that can be learned by almost anyone who has the desire and commitment to improve. The Leadership Practices Inventory Action Cards and activities were created to provide leaders with the opportunity to apply the LPI leadership behaviors to their own situations. Leadership is a learned skill, and the more opportunities leaders have to practice these skills, the more likely they are to be effective leaders.

The LPI Action Cards deck is comprised of thirty cards, each corresponding to one of the thirty LPI leadership behaviors. Each card has the behavior number, the behavior, and the leadership practice with which the behavior is associated. On the cards, the behaviors are written as they appear in the paper LPI and LPI Online. Due to space limitations, the LPI reports generated by the scoring software and LPI Online application utilize shorter phrases for some behaviors. Every effort is made to ensure that the correct meaning of the behavior is conveyed. The other identifying factors—the practice and number—remain the same. Facilitators may wish to explain these discrepancies at the commencement of a class or workshop. For example, a sample of a card is shown below.

1.

MODEL THE WAY

Sets a personal example of what he/she expects of others.

The activities in this guide represent just a few ways the LPI Action Cards might be used to help leaders practice effective leadership skills. We encourage leaders and facilitators to come up with other ways to use the cards to improve their leadership practices.

HOW TO USE THIS FACILITATOR'S GUIDE

Overall Flow of Activities

There are three types of LPI Action Card learning activities in this Guide:

- *Introductory Activities*—to introduce the concepts associated with the cards.
- *Application Activities*—to help leaders apply the concepts to their daily lives and work.
- *Reinforcement Activities*—to help leaders keep focused on the skills and behaviors required for their ongoing leadership development.

Activities are presented in the recommended order of delivery, and each activity has any prerequisite activities noted. The sequence of activities is

Introductory Activities
| Activity 1 | Leadership Behaviors Board Game |
| Activity 2 | Leaders Tell Us . . . |

Application Activities
Activity 3	Leadership Case Studies
Activity 4	Your Challenging Leadership Situation
Activity 5	LPI Action Card Shuffle
Activity 6	Aligning Actions with Leadership Behavior

Reinforcement Activities
Activity 7	Barriers and Tactics
Activity 8	Leadership Behavior Combinations
Activity 9	Feedback and Coaching Circle

Activity Design and Description

The design and description for the LPI Action Card activities includes:

- *Activity Overview*—A brief description of the activity
- *Purpose*—The purpose, objective(s), or outcome(s)
- *Participants*—Minimum, maximum, and best group size
- *Prerequisites*—Prerequisite LPI Action Card activities and recommended pre-work, if any
- *Time*—Recommended time for conducting the activity
- *Supplies and Resources*—Materials required
- *Facilitator Notes*—Sequence of events and instructions to the facilitator, including an overview, activity setup, introducing the activity, guidance for participants, debriefing and trigger questions, and the like
- *Variations*—Alternative ways to set up or conduct the activities
- *Coach's Notes*—Where appropriate, contains ideas for coaches who are working with individual leaders on how to adapt the activities to one-on-one interactions.

Suggestions for Successful Results

Planning and Preparing

This Facilitator's Guide walks you through the process of planning and delivering the LPI Action Card activities. It includes step-by-step instructions, and in some cases a "script" for setting up, conducting, and debriefing the activities. You can use the script as is or adapt it to meet the needs of your group.

Here are some suggestions for planning and preparing for successful results:

- Read this Facilitator's Guide carefully. The more familiar you are with the material, the easier it will be to facilitate its use with others.

- Think of stories and examples from your organization that you could use to further illustrate each of The Five Practices. This is particularly helpful in case study activities with the LPI Action Cards.

- Become more familiar with The Five Practices of Exemplary Leadership® model by reading *The Leadership Challenge,* which includes many stories to illustrate The Five Practices. Also visit www.leadershipchallenge.com for a wealth of information on the model, validity and reliability data, related materials, FAQs, facilitation tips and techniques, and more.

- Determine whether to make any changes to the activity design. For example, you may prefer to adjust the team size or time commitment in an activity. Any of the activities can become more indepth when you consider organizational examples, knowledge, and practice time. It is recommended that you spend the minimum suggested time allotted to get the most out of the activities.

- Notify participants. Send an invitation message to participants with details about the date, time, and location of the session. Tell them that the purpose is to introduce them to The Five Practices of Exemplary Leadership® or to deepen their leadership knowledge and skill.

- Arrange for the room and equipment you will need. Select a room in which participants will be comfortable and unlikely to be disturbed. These activities are designed to encourage interaction, so set the room up with tables arranged so participants can easily see you, any materials or flip charts, and each other. On the day of the session, arrive early enough to make sure that the room is set up properly and the equipment is in working order.

- Practice facilitating the activity. Walk through the activity until you are comfortable with the material, facilitating the activities, and so on.

- Another suggestion to make the most of these activities is to have participants choose "commitment partners." These partnerships are designed to give each participant a sounding board outside of the classroom to obtain feedback on how he/she is doing and what he/she might do differently. For example, commitment partners could be assigned at least one follow-up meeting after each activity, in which they would discuss specific questions or activities appropriate to their organization. The partnerships could be formed at the beginning of the first LPI Action Card activity for the group and last through all of the activities, or the make-up of the partnerships could change from one activity to the next. Considerations in choosing commitment partners include:

  - *Location:* Would it be beneficial for partners to be in the same location, or would you prefer to leverage relationships across locations?
  - *Department:* Are all participants from the same department? If not, how will you pair people? By department or across departments?
  - *Familiarity:* Would partners who know each other well be paired up, or would you prefer to expand participants' relationships by pairing up those who are less well acquainted?
  - *Frequency:* How frequently would you expect partners to meet or talk? Does that impact any of the other considerations listed?
  - *Commitment:* Will partners commit to themselves only, or will you formalize the partnerships and create a reporting mechanism for them to report back to the group and/or facilitator?

During the Session

Here are some suggestions to keep the activities on track during the session:

- *Watch the time.* The times given in this Facilitator's Guide are estimates. Keep things moving. Bring discussions and activities to a close when time is up.
- *Manage discussions.* Keep discussions focused on the topic at hand. If participants veer off topic, bring them back. If they begin to repeat themselves, summarize the discussion and move on to the next topic.
- *Encourage participants to contribute their own stories.* The more participants can relate the content of an activity to their own experiences and situations, the more useful the time will be to them. Encourage them to share their own experiences and discuss ways the concepts relate to their organizations.

Follow-Up

Many activities will include suggested follow-ups. However, creating your own follow-ups, based on what will be successful in your organization, is encouraged. The more often the concepts are reinforced to leaders, the stronger their leadership will become. For example, you might send out *The Leadership Challenge Newsletter,* or sign up your leaders for the newsletter (see resources below), or schedule follow-up meetings two weeks after each activity. These can be brief, but they will go a long way in reinforcing what leaders have learned since the activity.

SUCCESSFUL RESULTS

The best way to become familiar with this Facilitator's Guide is to start to use the activities with leaders in your organization. By preparing for and delivering the activities, you will understand what works for you and your leaders, as well as areas in which you might want to customize them for your organization. You may also want to follow up with those who have participated in the activities. By following up with participants, you can obtain feedback on the activities, as well as hear how their leadership behaviors have changed or improved.

ADDITIONAL RESOURCES

James M. Kouzes and Barry Z. Posner. *The Leadership Challenge* (4th ed.).
San Francisco: Jossey-Bass, 2007.

The Leadership Challenge website (www.leadershipchallenge.com) offers a number of introductory articles, including the following website headings:

- "About *The Leadership Challenge*" includes the history of TLC, the approach, and video interviews of the authors.
- "Research" includes research by the authors, as well as hundreds of other research papers using the *Leadership Practices Inventory* as a tool for measurement.
- "Expand Your Skills" includes a section on "Tips & Techniques" for using the five practices.
- "Ask the Expert," which has common questions answered by experts on *The Leadership Challenge*, "Recommended Reading," and the "TLC Newsletter" are also housed under this heading.

INTRODUCTORY ACTIVITIES

Activity 1: Leadership Behaviors Board Game

Activity 2: Leaders Tell Us . . .*

ACTIVITY 1
LEADERSHIP BEHAVIORS
BOARD GAME

ACTIVITY OVERVIEW

Participants use the LPI cards and "Leadership Opportunity" scenarios to play a fun and lively game for building knowledge of the LPI behaviors.

PURPOSE

The purpose of this activity is to provide an opportunity to learn more about the LPI behaviors in a fun way. As a result of this activity, participants will be able to:

- Identify the thirty LPI behaviors and how they make up The Five Practices of Exemplary Leadership®.

PARTICIPANTS

Minimum: 2 per game board
Maximum: 5 per game board
Recommended: 3 to 5 per game board
  (Participants are divided into groups/teams of three to five. Avoid forming teams larger than five members to maintain the timing of the game.)

PREREQUISITE

None

TIME

45 to 60 minutes; includes setup, the activity, and debriefing

SUPPLIES AND RESOURCES

- LPI Action Card deck for each group (one to two decks, depending on whether the Variation is used)
- Leadership Behaviors Board Game for each group
- Leadership Opportunity Cards and Game Pieces for each group
- One die for each group (not included)
- The Leadership Practices and Commitments handout (number 1) for each participant
- The Thirty Leadership Behaviors handout (number 2) for each participant
- LPI Action Card deck for each participant to take away

FACILITATOR NOTES

Activity Setup

- Divide participants into equal-sized groups of three to five members each. Seat group members around a table.
- Distribute Leadership Behaviors Board Game, LPI Action Cards, Leadership Opportunity Cards, colored game pieces for each participant, and one die to each group.
- Distribute The Leadership Practices and Commitments handout (number 1) to each participant.
- Distribute The Thirty Leadership Behaviors handout (number 2) to each participant.

Overview

(Note: If participants have not yet taken the Leadership Practices Inventory or been introduced to The Leadership Challenge, provide a brief overview. Refer to the Introduction to this Facilitator's Guide for a general introduction, adding your own experience and understanding.)

To begin, say the following in your own words:

- While many would contend that leadership is something that you are "born with" or not, Kouzes and Posner believe, and research shows, that leadership is learned. Based on their research, they've developed the Leadership Practices Inventory (LPI), which surveys leaders and their constituents specifically about the thirty behaviors that make up The Five Practices of Exemplary Leadership®: Model the Way, Inspire a Shared Vision, Challenge the Process, Enable Others to Act, and Encourage the Heart.
- Today we will begin to learn these thirty LPI behaviors through a board game. The purpose of this activity is to provide an opportunity to learn more about the LPI behaviors in a fun way. As a result of this activity, you will be able to identify the thirty LPI behaviors and how they make up The Five Practices of Exemplary Leadership®.

Introduce the Activity

Review the following instructions before beginning play.

- *The object of the game is for you to move your game piece on the game board by matching the LPI behaviors to their respective Leadership Practices. The first player to reach "Finish" wins the game.*
- *Each player will choose a game piece (marked Leader 1 to 5) and place it on "Start." Each player will roll the die to decide who goes first. The game will then rotate to the first player's left. The LPI Action Cards and the Leadership Opportunity Cards should be shuffled and set face down to the side of the game board.*

- *Our game will take about forty-five minutes to play, so let's get started!*

Play the Game

Give the following game instructions:

1. *The first player rolls the die. The player to his or her right draws an LPI Action Card and reads the **behavior only** aloud. The first player then states which leadership practice that LPI behavior supports.*
2. *If the other players believe that the answer in not correct, they may challenge the player's answer. Start with the player to the first player's left and quickly ask each if he or she challenges the answer. After everyone has had the chance to challenge, the card holder provides the correct leadership practice.*
3. *If the initial player is correct in matching the leadership behavior to the leadership practice on the card, the player moves his or her game piece ahead on the game board the number of spaces on the die.*
4. *If a challenging player is correct, the first challenger to give the correct answer moves ahead the number of spaces on the die; the original player moves back one space.*
5. *If the both original and the challenging players are incorrect, they each move back one space. The LPI Action Card is moved to the bottom of the deck and the game rotates to the next player on the left.*
6. *There's one more set of cards: the Leadership Opportunity Cards. When a player lands on a star, the player draws one of the Leadership Opportunity Cards. These cards have scenarios to which a leadership practice could be applied. The player reads the card aloud and does as it says, and then either moves back or moves ahead as instructed. Here is an example:*
   - *At a meeting with your manager, you felt a tinge of uneasiness and decided not to share your idea. You should*

have Challenged the Process, but you decided not to take the risk. Move back two spaces.

Complete the Activity

After reviewing the rules and the flow of the game, practice the game with one LPI Action Card, without anyone receiving points. (Note: demonstrate the game with an LPI Action Card, answering questions as needed.). Once everyone is clear on the rules, allow each group to complete the game to identify a winner.

Debrief

Ask participants the following questions, and probe for more information when necessary:

- *Who are the winners at each table?* (Have participants give the winners a round of applause!)
- *No matter who won the game, the object of this game was to help you learn and apply the LPI behaviors. What have you learned about how the LPI behaviors relate to the five practices?*
- *How were the Leadership Opportunity Cards related to the practices? To the behaviors? What did you learn about how to apply the behaviors to these opportunities?*
- *How can you apply what you learned today about the leadership behaviors to some real leadership situations you are facing?*

Wrap Up

As we noted when we began, leadership is learned. By using the thirty leadership behaviors, leaders are able to Model the Way, Inspire a Shared Vision, Challenge the Process, Enable Others to Act, and Encourage the Heart.

Our game today helped you learn more about the LPI behaviors. You should be more comfortable now identifying the thirty LPI behaviors and how they make up the Five Practices of Exemplary Leadership®. We also have a visual reminder for you. As you move ahead, look for leadership opportunities to apply what you learned today. To become more familiar with the leadership behaviors, review the handout I'm going to give you, as well as the LPI Action Cards I will give you. If you've completed the Leadership Practices Inventory, use the cards in conjunction with your leadership behavior ranking from the report.

Thank the group for their participation.

- Distribute the Thirty Leadership Behaviors Handout (number 2).
- Distribute one LPI Action Card deck per participant if they do not yet have their own decks.

VARIATION

To challenge participants further, have them link situations with specific leadership behaviors and practices. Have a second deck of Leadership Action Cards on hand, with the cards organized by leadership practice. After a Leadership Opportunity card is drawn and the correct practice has been given, challenge the player to review the cards from the practice(s) mentioned and determine which behavior(s) could be applied in the opportunity. See the Answer Key below for the **best** answer(s) to each leadership opportunity, and allow discussion if other answers are given, as they may apply as well.

Answer Key:
Leadership Opportunity Card
Correct Leadership Behaviors

1. 8: Challenges people to try new approaches (Challenge)

2. 1. Sets a personal example of what is expected (Model)
   26. Is clear about his/her philosophy of leadership (Model)

3. 9: Actively listens to diverse points of view (Enable)

4. 26. Is clear about his/her philosophy of leadership (Model)

5. 30. Gives team members appreciation and support (Encourage)
    5. Praises people for a job well done (Encourage)

6. 14. Treat others with dignity and respect (Enable)
    4. Develops cooperative relationships (Enable)
    1. Sets a personal example of what is expected (Model)
    9. Actively listens to diverse points of view (Enable)

7. 9. Actively listens to diverse points of view (Enable)
    14. Treat others with dignity and respect (Enable)

8. 30. Gives team members appreciation and support (Encourage)
    5. Praises people for a job well done (Encourage)

9. 1. Sets a personal example of what is expected (Model)

10. 10. Expresses confidence in people's abilities (Encourage)
    27. Speaks with conviction about meaning of work

11. 7. Describes a compelling image of the future
    22. Paints a big picture of group aspirations

12. 26. Is clear about his/her philosophy of leadership
    21. Builds consensus around the organization's values

13. 12. Appeals to other to share dream of the future
    17. Shows others how their interests can be realized

14. 23. Makes certain that goals, plans, and milestones are set

COACH'S NOTES

If you are working one-on-one with a leader, you can adapt this activity. While the game board may not be best suited for coaching a leader, you might use the Opportunity Cards as they are used in the Variation above to help the leader become more familiar with the leadership behaviors.

You might also have the leader share similar situations that he/she has been in and discuss how the behaviors in the answer key could be used to address those situations.

HANDOUT 1
THE LEADERSHIP PRACTICES AND COMMITMENTS

Model the Way

1. Clarify values by finding your voice and affirming shared ideals.
2. Set the example by aligning actions and shared values.

Inspire a Shared Vision

3. Envision the future by imagining exciting and ennobling possibilities.
4. Enlist others in a common vision by appealing to shared aspirations.

Challenge the Process

5. Search for opportunities by seizing the initiative and by looking outward for innovative ways to improve.
6. Experiment and take risks by constantly generating small wins and learning from experience.

Enable Others to Act

7. Foster collaboration by building trust and facilitating relationships.
8. Strengthen others by increasing self-determination and developing competence.

Encourage the Heart

9. Recognize contributions by showing appreciation for individual excellence.
10. Celebrate the values and victories by creating a spirit of community.

Leadership Practices Inventory (LPI) Action Cards
Copyright © 2010 by James M. Kouzes and Barry Z. Posner.
Reproduced by permission of Pfeiffer, an Imprint of Wiley. www.pfeiffer.com.

Handouts/Materials

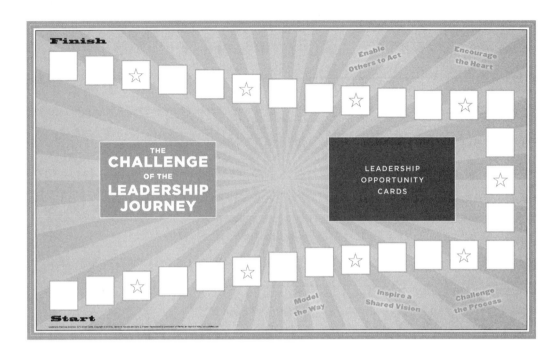

Leadership Opportunity Cards

Print one to five copies of this document on card stock, depending on the number of teams you have. Cut out the cards, shuffle, and place on the Game Board.

1. At a meeting with your manager, you felt a tinge of uneasiness and decided not to share your idea. You should have **Challenged the Process,** but you decided not to take the risk.

Move back 2 spaces.

2. To build stronger relationship with your team, you wrote a "credo memo" based on your personal values and shared it with your team. **You Modeled the Way!**

Move ahead 4 spaces.

3. You had a lot you wanted to share at the meeting and made sure every-one knew your perspective, but you did not listen to their feedback. You could have **Enabled Others to Act.**

Move back 2 spaces.

4. You started with the reflection question: What really matters to me? From there, you became clear about your personal values. **Model the Way** begins with self-reflection.

Move ahead 4 spaces.

5. During a recent conversation with your team, you did not give en-couragement because it felt awkward to you. Besides, they knew they did a good job anyway. You could have **Encouraged the Heart.**

Move back 3 spaces.

6. Give your game partners one good reason why it's not a leadership behavior to blame others when you disagree with them. That's not **Modeling the Way** and **Enabling Other to Act!**

Move ahead 2 spaces.

7. When suggesting a work improve-ment, you ignored the ideas of others at a meeting. The others left the meeting thinking you did not treat others with dignity and respect. You did not **Enable Others to Act.**

Move back 4 spaces.

8. You let your team know why you appreciate their efforts and how their actions make a difference. You know the value of **Encouraging the Heart.**

Move ahead 3 spaces.

Leadership Opportunity Cards

Print one to five copies of this document on card stock, depending on the number of teams you have. Cut out the cards, shuffle, and place on the Game Board.

9. You often become so busy and behind with what you said you will do that you find it difficult to keep promises and commitments. You need to focus on how you can **Model the Way.**

Move back 2 spaces.

10. It's important to help your team see the value they bring, and you often share your conviction about the meaning of their work. That **Inspires a Shared Vision** for everyone!

Move ahead 3 spaces.

11. You think this "vision thing" is the responsibility of the senior management, not you. They are the ones who should **Inspire a Shared Vision.**

Move back 4 spaces.

12. You recently shared how important you think teamwork is to your group and others.

Move ahead 3 spaces.

13. In challenging times, it is far more important to be a manager than to be a leader.

Move back 3 spaces.

14. Your team members are always asking what your plans and timelines are for projects. You think they should just set them on their own.

Move back 2 spaces.

Game Pieces

Print one to five copies of this document, depending on the number of teams you have. Cut out the game pieces and distribute to the players.

Leadership Practices Inventory (LPI) Action Cards Copyright © 2010 by James M. Kouzes and Barry Z. Posner. Reproduced by permission of Pfeiffer, an imprint of Wiley. www.pfeiffer.com

25

HANDOUT 2
THE THIRTY LEADERSHIP BEHAVIORS

The Five Practices of Exemplary Leadership	The Thirty Leadership Behaviors
Model the Way	1. Sets a personal example of what he/she expects of others.
	6. Makes certain that people adhere to agreed-on standards.
	11. Follows through on promises and commitments.
	16. Asks for feedback for how his/her actions affect people's performance.
	21. Builds consensus around organization's values.
	26. Is clear about his/her philosophy of leadership.
Inspire a Shared Vision	2. Talks about future trends influencing our work.
	7. Describes a compelling image of the future.
	12. Appeals to others to share dream of the future.
	17. Shows others how their interests can be realized.
	22. Paints "big picture" of group aspirations.
	27. Speaks with conviction about the meaning of work.

Leadership Practices Inventory (LPI) Action Cards
Copyright © 2010 by James M. Kouzes and Barry Z. Posner.
Reproduced by permission of Pfeiffer, an Imprint of Wiley. www.pfeiffer.com.

The Five Practices of Exemplary Leadership	The Thirty Leadership Behaviors
Challenge the Process	3. Seeks challenging opportunities to test skills.
	8. Challenges people to try new approaches.
	13. Searches outside organization for innovative ways to improve.
	18. Asks "What can we learn?"
	23. Makes certain that goals, plans, and milestones are set.
	28. Experiments and takes risks.
Enable Others to Act	4. Develops cooperative relationships.
	9. Actively listens to diverse points of view.
	14. Treats people with dignity and respect.
	19. Supports decisions other people make.
	24. Gives people choice about how to do their work.
	29. Ensures that people grow in their jobs.
Encourage the Heart	5. Praises people for a job well done.
	10. Expresses confidence in people's abilities.
	15. Creatively rewards people for their contributions.
	20. Recognizes people for commitment to shared values.
	25. Finds ways to celebrate accomplishments.
	30. Gives team members appreciation and support.

ACTIVITY 2
LEADERS TELL US . . .*

ACTIVITY OVERVIEW

This is a drawing game, similar to Win, Lose, or Draw and Pictionary®. Participants use the LPI Action Cards to pick leadership behaviors that they will draw for their teams. Teams that guess correctly win points while learning the LPI behaviors.

PURPOSE

The purpose of this activity is to provide an opportunity to learn more about the LPI behaviors in a fun way and practice creating visual imagery, which is key for Inspiring a Shared Vision.

As a result of this activity, participants will be able to:

- Identify the thirty LPI behaviors and how they make up The Five Practices of Exemplary Leadership®.
- Illustrate the behaviors in a visual way.

PARTICIPANTS

Minimum: 4
Maximum: 40
Recommended: 10 to 14
(Participants are divided into two to four groups.)

PREREQUISITE

None

Adapted from an activity originally implemented by Jim Kouzes and Barry Posner.

TIME

30 to 60 minutes (depending on time available); includes setup, the activity, and debriefing

SUPPLIES AND RESOURCES

- LPI Action Card deck for each group
- Leaders Tell Us . . . Scoring Sheet
- Die, timer, pencil, flip-chart markers for each group (not provided)
- Also needed are large sheets of paper, masking tape, and/or easel pads.
- The Leadership Practices and Commitments handout (number 1) for each participant
- The Thirty Leadership Behaviors handout (number 2) for each participant
- One LPI Action Card deck for each participant to take away

FACILITATOR NOTES

Activity Setup

- Form two teams by dividing players into teams of equal number. If there are more than twenty people playing, form three teams. Form four teams with thirty-one to forty people playing. Ideally, each team will have fewer than ten participants.
- Distribute a timer, markers, and a deck of LPI Action Cards to each team.
- Distribute The Leadership Practices and Commitments handout, one per participant.
- Distribute The Thirty Leadership Behaviors handout to all participants.

(Note: If participants are very familiar with The Leadership Challenge and the thirty leadership behaviors, you might consider adding difficulty to the activity by not distributing the handouts.)

Overview

(Note: If participants have not yet taken the Leadership Practices Inventory or been introduced to The Leadership Challenge, provide a brief overview. Refer to the Introduction to this Facilitator's Guide for a general introduction, adding your own experience and understanding. You may also want to provide The Leadership Practices and Commitments handout as a visual reminder.)

Share the following with participants:

"While many would contend that leadership is something that you are 'born with' or not, Kouzes and Posner believe, and research shows, that leadership is learned. Based on their research, they've developed the Leadership Practices Inventory (LPI), *which surveys leaders and their constituents specifically about the thirty behaviors that make up The Five Practices of Exemplary Leadership®: Model the Way, Inspire a Shared Vision, Challenge the Process, Enable Others to Act, and Encourage the Heart.*

"Today we will begin to learn these thirty LPI behaviors through a game. The purpose of this activity is to provide an opportunity to learn more about the LPI behaviors in a fun way and to practice creating visual imagery, which is key for Inspiring a Shared Vision. As a result of this activity, you will be able to identify the thirty LPI behaviors and how they make up The Five Practices of Exemplary Leadership®, and you will have some great practice at illustrating the behaviors in a visual way."

Introduce the Activity

Review the following instructions before beginning play.

- *High die roll decides which team plays first. The first team selects a "lead drawer"; all other first team players are then the "guessers." As one team draws and guesses the phrase on the LPI Action Card, the opposing team watches. Play alternates between teams with each new phrase to be drawn.*
- *Rotate the role of lead drawer on a team so that all team members have the opportunity to be the lead drawer.*

Play the Game

State the following rules of the game before beginning the play:

1. *The lead drawer secretly looks at the first card in the game deck. On each game card is an LPI behavior—for example, "challenges people to try new approaches."*
2. *The lead drawer turns over the timer and the countdown (3 minutes) begins. This is the time limit, kept track of by the opposing team.*
3. *The lead drawer then sketches out a picture clue or clues of the leadership behavior on the card. This could include the leadership practice that the behavior defines. For example, a clue for number 14, "Treats people with dignity and respect" could be Enable Others to Act.*
4. *As the lead drawer sketches, her/his teammates start shouting out what they think is being drawn. Players can guess as many times as they want. Guessing is not done in turn!*
5. Explain the drawing rules:
   - *Focus on the key concept of the behavior.*
   - *No letters, words or numbers can be drawn. Symbols such as dollar signs ($), arrows (>), etc., are acceptable.*
   - *If part of the behavior is guessed correctly, you may write that word next to your sketch.*
   - *Never speak while drawing, but you may gesture to indicate whether the guess is close or off-track.*

Sample Drawing for "Leaders Tell Us..."

① Practice: <u>Enable Others To Act</u>

② Behavior: <u>Treats</u> <u>people</u> <u>____</u>

<u>____</u> <u>and</u> <u>____</u>

people

sounds like:

= and

Answer: Treats people w/
Dignity + Respect

<u>trick</u> or <u>treats</u>

- *You may also draw an ear [pull on your ear] to mean "sounds like" and then draw a rhyming word.*
- *You may draw a series of dashes (– – – –) to indicate how many words are in the LPI behavior stated on your card. Draw a vertical line through the dash to indicate the number of syllables in the word (e.g., –/–/– for lead-er-ship).*

6. Explain the scoring:
   - *If the lead drawer's team guesses correctly before the time has elapsed, this team gets 1 point and marks the score on the scoring sheet.*
   - *If the lead drawer's team does not guess correctly before the time is elapsed, the team does not earn a point. The second team then has ten seconds to make one guess to win the point. (This opportunity continues in turn until all remaining teams have made one guess.) If the opposing team does guess correctly, they receive 1 point.*

7. Once the point has been played, the next team selects a new lead drawer and play begins again.

Complete the Activity

After reviewing the rules and the flow of the game, begin play. Play as many rounds as your allotted time will permit. At the end of the game, the team with the most points wins.

Debrief

Ask participants the following questions, and probe for more information when necessary:

- *What did you learn about the Leadership Practices Inventory behaviors?*
- *Was it difficult or easy to draw these behaviors? Why or why not?*
- *How familiar were you with the behaviors? Would drawing be easier the more familiar you were with them?*

Wrap Up

Say: "*The purpose of this activity was to provide an opportunity to learn more about the LPI behaviors in a fun way and practice creating visual imagery, which is key for Inspiring a Shared Vision. Now you can identify the thirty LPI behaviors and how they make up The Five Practices of Exemplary Leadership®. Thinking about them through pictures is a great way for you to recall them as you develop and practice your leadership skills. Having the behaviors "top-of-mind" will allow you to focus your development on specific behaviors, increasing your use, and therefore improving your leadership.*"

Distribute one LPI Action Card deck per participant if they do not yet have their own decks.

Thank the group for their participation.

VARIATIONS

1. **Learning Aid:** Many of the Leadership Behaviors are conceptual and may be hard for some to draw. You may want to allow participant to use The Thirty Leadership Behaviors handout or their own LPI turned to the Leadership Behaviors Ranking page as a tip sheet.

2. **Individual Play:** Playing individually is a good solution if you have a small number of participants. In this variation, two to four participants can play. Each participant is one team.
   - First have participants write the individuals' names in the first row of the Leaders Tell Us . . . Score Card. For example, Steve would be listed in the space with Team 1, Kristen with Team 2, etc.
   - The drawing player draws for all others to guess.
   - When someone guesses the clue correctly, both the drawer and the guesser mark 1 point in the corresponding space. If no one guesses the clue, no points are given.
   - The player with the most points at the end of the game wins.

3. **Independent Drawing:** A third option is to have participants work independently for ten minutes to draw a visual representation of the behavior and practice on action cards that they pull from the deck.

   • Provide a sheet of flip-chart paper, markers, and masking tape to each participant.

   • Have each participant draw from the LPI Action Card deck and allow ten to fifteen minutes for them to draw the behavior/ practice on the bottom two-thirds of the chart paper.

   • After each person has competed a drawing, post the flip charts around the room and allow participants to go around the room to try to identify which behavior/practice has been drawn on each page. Have them write their guesses with their names on the top third of the flip-chart pages, allowing room for other guesses. (Amount of time allowed will vary by the number of participants.)

   • Have participants return to where their own drawings are and share what the behavior/practices were in their drawings.

   • Track who had the most correct guesses to determine the winner.

COACH'S NOTES

If you are working one-on-one with a leader, you can adapt this activity in a number of ways. While there is obviously no need to keep points, this activity provides the leader with visual reminders of the LPI leadership behaviors that he/she creates. You may decide to select only one card per session to draw, focusing on the behavior you are coaching to in that session. Assigning the drawing as pre-work prior to your coaching session is a good idea to allow reflection time. (You may want to specify whether you prefer a large drawing on flip-chart paper or a drawing on a blank 8½-by-11-inch sheet of paper.) The leader should spend no more than thirty minutes on the drawing. Your assignment can be based on upcoming coaching topics, or on one of the following options:

1. **Top Ten and Bottom Ten:** If the leader has completed the *Leadership Practices Inventory*, you might focus on his/her top and bottom ten ranked LPI behaviors, having the leader select a card from each of those areas to draw. Focusing on the top ten ranked behaviors can help leaders recognize and leverage their strengths. If the leader has not yet completed the LPI survey, suggest that he/she review the cards and draw one of the ten behaviors he/she uses most frequently and one of the ten behaviors he/she uses less frequently.

2. **Draw a Practice:** Have the leader draw the entire practice that he/she needs to work on most. He/She can draw the practice and each of the six behaviors or create a drawing that simply captures the entire practice. The key is to create a visual reminder that will help the leader focus on the practice and the behaviors. For example, if Encourage the Heart is the leader's lowest practice, have him/her create a drawing that symbolizes the practice and the behaviors that he/she wants to focus on for improvement.

3. **Practice Inspire a Shared Vision:** For many leaders, Inspire a Shared Vision is their lowest among the five practices and the most difficult to impact. Since Inspire is all about "painting the picture," this would be an excellent practice to capture in an image (and the act of drawing it gives the leader more practice at the behaviors!). The leader can focus on the behaviors that are of most interest to him/her. Leaders may also choose to focus on the following behaviors, as these are the more visual of the six behaviors:
   - Behavior 7: Describes a compelling image of the future
   - Behavior 22: Paints "big picture" of group aspirations

   Have the leader post his/her drawing in the work area. You may want to make a copy of the drawing for your records as well.

LEADERS TELL US . . . SCORING SHEET

Scoring for Team Play

1. Write the names of the players on each team in the areas provided.

2. If the drawing team guesses correctly before the time has elapsed, the team earns 1 point and marks it in the space that corresponds to the current round. Each team repeats this step throughout each round.

3. If the drawing team does not guess correctly, each other team, in succession, has ten seconds to guess. The first team to guess correctly earns the point.

Scoring for Individual Play

1. If playing with two to four individuals instead of in a team, write the *individuals'* names in the first row. For example, Steve would be listed in the space with Team 1, Kristen with Team 2, etc.

2. The drawing player draws for all others to guess. When someone guesses the clue correctly, both the drawer and the guesser mark 1 point in the corresponding space. If no one guesses the clue correctly, no points are given.

Name:				
Round	Team 1 Team Member Names:*	Team 2 Team Member Names:*	Team 3 Team Member Names:*	Team 4 Team Member Names:*
1				
2				
3				
4				
5				
6				
7				
8				
Total Scores:				

* Optional

HANDOUT 1
THE LEADERSHIP PRACTICES
AND COMMITMENTS

Model the Way

1. Clarify values by finding your voice and affirming shared ideals.
2. Set the example by aligning actions and shared values.

Inspire a Shared Vision

3. Envision the future by imagining exciting and ennobling possibilities.

4. Enlist others in a common vision by appealing to shared aspirations.

Challenge the Process

5. Search for opportunities by seizing the initiative and by looking outward for innovative ways to improve.

6. Experiment and take risks by constantly generating small wins and learning from experience.

Enable Others to Act

7. Foster collaboration by building trust and facilitating relationships.

8. Strengthen others by increasing self-determination and developing competence.

Encourage the Heart

9. Recognize contributions by showing appreciation for individual excellence.

10. Celebrate the values and victories by creating a spirit of community.

Leadership Practices Inventory (LPI) Action Cards
Copyright © 2010 by James M. Kouzes and Barry Z. Posner.
Reproduced by permission of Pfeiffer, an Imprint of Wiley. www.pfeiffer.com.

HANDOUT 2
THE THIRTY LEADERSHIP BEHAVIORS

The Five Practices of Exemplary Leadership	The Thirty Leadership Behaviors
Model the Way	1. Sets a personal example of what he/she expects of others.
	6. Makes certain that people adhere to agreed-on standards.
	11. Follows through on promises and commitments.
	16. Asks for feedback for how his/her actions affect people's performance.
	21. Builds consensus around organization's values.
	26. Is clear about his/her philosophy of leadership.
Inspire a Shared Vision	2. Talks about future trends influencing our work.
	7. Describes a compelling image of the future.
	12. Appeals to others to share dream of the future.
	17. Shows others how their interests can be realized.
	22. Paints "big picture" of group aspirations.
	27. Speaks with conviction about the meaning of work.

(Continued)

Leadership Practices Inventory (LPI) Action Cards
Copyright © 2010 by James M. Kouzes and Barry Z. Posner.
Reproduced by permission of Pfeiffer, an Imprint of Wiley. www.pfeiffer.com.

The Five Practices of Exemplary Leadership	The Thirty Leadership Behaviors
Challenge the Process	3. Seeks challenging opportunities to test skills.
	8. Challenges people to try new approaches.
	13. Searches outside organization for innovative ways to improve.
	18. Asks "What can we learn?"
	23. Makes certain that goals, plans, and milestones are set.
	28. Experiments and takes risks.
Enable Others to Act	4. Develops cooperative relationships.
	9. Actively listens to diverse points of view.
	14. Treats people with dignity and respect.
	19. Supports decisions other people make.
	24. Gives people choice about how to do their work.
	29. Ensures that people grow in their jobs.
Encourage the Heart	5. Praises people for a job well done.
	10. Expresses confidence in people's abilities.
	15. Creatively rewards people for their contributions.
	20. Recognizes people for commitment to shared values.
	25. Finds ways to celebrate accomplishments.
	30. Gives team members appreciation and support.

APPLICATION ACTIVITIES

Activity 3: Leadership Case Studies

Activity 4: Your Challenging Leadership Situation

Activity 5: LPI Action Card Shuffle

Activity 6: Aligning Actions with Leadership Behavior

ACTIVITY 3
LEADERSHIP CASE STUDIES

ACTIVITY OVERVIEW

In this activity, participants will work in small groups to play a card game for which the object is to select thirty LPI Action Cards to assess and resolve case studies with leadership dilemmas.

PURPOSE

Help participants learn the *Leadership Practices Inventory* behaviors and use them in a case study situation so that they can apply them at a future date to their own leadership challenges. Participants will be able to:

- Use the thirty LPI behaviors to apply specific actions to workplace issues for which they need to see improved results
- Use LPI Action Cards on their own and with their teams or others for future workplace issue resolution

PARTICIPANTS

Minimum: 3
Maximum: None
Recommended: 12 to 15
   (Participants work in groups of three to five in this activity.)

PREREQUISITE

Familiarity with LPI behaviors. Suggested pre-work includes introductory activities such as Leaders Tell Us . . . and the Leadership Behaviors Board Game, as well as completion of the *Leadership Practices Inventory*.

TIME

1 hour and 15 minutes, which includes setup, the activity, and debriefing

SUPPLIES AND RESOURCES

- LPI Action Card deck for each group
- LPI Action Card deck for each participant to take away
- Leadership Case Studies handout (number 3) for each participant
- Our Real Work Situations and LPI Behaviors Application handout (number 4) for each participant

(*Note:* Before this activity, have the LPI Action Cards and hand-outs ready to provide to participants.)

FACILITATOR NOTES

Overview

The LPI leadership behaviors provide a rich starting point for leadership development. Whether or not participants have completed the *Leadership Practices Inventory,* they can use the LPI leadership behaviors to focus their development. Applying the behaviors to real-life situations deepens one's understanding of the behaviors and how they can influence positive outcomes for leaders and those around them.

In this activity, case studies will enable participants to learn the *Leadership Practices Inventory* behaviors so that they can begin to apply them to their own leadership challenges. As a result, they should be able to apply specific actions to the thirty LPI behaviors and use LPI Action Cards in the future on their own and with their teams or with other leaders to resolve any number of issues that come up in the course of their daily work. Leaders should apply these behaviors to work on projects, to improve performance and quality, and to help meet their goals and targets. These behaviors can be applied to ANY workplace issue a leader experiences.

Activity Setup

- Divide participants into table groups of three to five. Ask them to sit at their tables so they can play a card game, with the table clear of materials and other workshop items.
- Distribute one deck of LPI Action cards per table.
- Distribute the Leadership Case Studies handout to each participant.

Introduce the Activity

Have participants read Case Study 1 and have a brief table discussion about the key points noted in Questions 1 through 4 on the handout. Have participants take notes on their handouts. Allow ten to fifteen minutes.

- What are the themes of this workplace challenge, issue, or situation?
- Who is impacted as a result of the challenge, issue, or situation?
- How does the challenge, issue, or situation affect relationships?
- How does the challenge, issue, or situation affect organization/unit/team results?

Once they have read and discussed Case Study 1, the participants will have an opportunity to share their ideas about how to handle this situation with their table groups using the LPI behaviors in a fun and meaningful activity.

Playing the Game

For the first round, provide the following instructions one step at a time to get the groups accustomed to the process they will use for the activity. Afterward, they will cycle the rounds on their own.

- Step 1: Each team selects a dealer. The dealer shuffles the cards and deals them out to everyone in the table group. Deal out all the cards in the deck. Some individuals may have more cards than others. *(Step 1 takes about one minute.)*

- Step 2: Each person reviews his/her "hand." Notice that each card has three identifications—the number of the LPI behavior, one of the five leadership practices and the specific LPI behavior that relates to the number. Each participant mentally selects one of the behaviors from the LPI Action Cards in his or her hand that could help address the situation/problem in the case study. *(Step 2 takes three or four minutes.)*
- Step 3: Starting with the person to the left of the dealer, each participant takes a turn by placing the selected LPI Action Card in the center of the table. Each player reads the LPI behavior number and leadership behavior aloud and explains how this behavior can address the situation. Each participant should place one card in the center of the table. *(Step 3 takes six to eight minutes.)*
- Step 4: Once your group is finished, complete Question 5 from the Leadership Case Studies handout, including an action plan using the LPI behaviors you identified. Often there are one or two behaviors that are most applicable as first steps to resolving the issue. These should appear first in the action plan. *(Step 4 takes five minutes.)*
- Step 5: Debrief Round 1/first case study with all table groups, using Questions 6, 7, and 8 on the Leadership Case Studies handout.

Complete the Activity

Have the table groups start Round 2 and repeat Steps 1 through 5 with a new case study. Tell them to choose new dealers. Afterward, continue with rounds until all the table groups have completed Steps 1 through 5 for each of the three case studies.

Debrief

Ask participants the following questions, and probe for more information when necessary:

- *How did the situations in the case studies compare to those in your own workplace?*
- *What did you learn about applying the leadership behaviors to specific workplace situations?*
- *What were some of the leadership behaviors that you were able to apply?*
- *Do you find yourself applying this in the regular course of your day now? Why or why not?*
- *How might you apply these or other behaviors to your own workplace situations?*

Wrap Up

The focus for this activity was to learn more about the LPI leadership behaviors and use them in a case study situation so that leaders can apply them at a future date to their own leadership challenges. They now have practice at using the thirty LPI behaviors and can use them on their own, with other leaders, or with their teams to improve overall leadership and results.

Encourage participants to be observant of their own leadership challenges, issues, and situations and to think through the list of questions on their own. They should also share the LPI behaviors with their work teams, peers, and managers to tackle real workplace issues as they arise, using them as solutions.

Thank the group for their participation.

- Distribute Our Real Work Situations and LPI Behaviors Application (Handout 4).
- Distribute one LPI Action Card deck per participant if they do not yet have their own decks.

VARIATIONS

1. **Case Study by Group:** If you are short on time, participants can be divided into three groups, each focusing on one of the case studies. Since participants will have the opportunity to review only one case, allowing each group to share its case and conclusions in the debriefing is important. Ask each group to select a spokesperson to briefly share:
   - The scenario
   - The most important leadership behavior
   - The action they would take with that behavior

2. **Three Meetings:** If short amounts of time are available over a period, participants can focus on one case study per meeting. This also allows reinforcement of the leadership behaviors over time as well as practice using the cards. It creates a "coaching circle" wherein leaders coach and are coached by each other.

3. **Take a Different Perspective:** Assigning one of several perspectives deepens the analysis of the case studies. (*Note:* The depth of discussion in this option may require adding time to the activity.)
   - This variation works best in groups of three.
   - For example, participants are asked to take one of the following perspectives in analyzing the issue (you may add those that are appropriate to your environment):
     - Manager
     - Peer
     - Human Resources Director
     - Direct Report
     - Customer (Internal or External)
   - From this perspective they choose the LPI Action Cards they think most appropriate. For example, if looking from the perspective of a direct report in Case Study 1, a participant may choose number 14, "Treats people with dignity and

respect" rather than number 8, "Challenges people to take new approaches," because in a restructuring, a direct report is looking at how people are treated and may not want to be challenged at such a time.

- Debrief the activity, asking those who took each perspective to report how they viewed the challenge differently. Ask:
  - *How did your perspective impact the leadership behaviors that you chose?*
  - *In what kinds of situations may you want to take on these different perspectives in order to analyze an issue?*
    (Bonus! What behavior does this represent? Number 9, "Actively listens to diverse points of view.")
- If focusing on one case only, end here. If focusing on all three cases, either divide participants among three teams or have group members switch roles for each of the three cases.

4. **Role Play:** Allowing leaders to role play using the leadership behaviors provides a way for leaders to practice in a controlled environment. Speaking the words they would use in an actual situation challenges leaders and provides a great learning opportunity. To create a role play at the end of the case studies based on the roles demonstrated in Variation 3 above, follow the steps below.
   - Logistics:
     - To offer each participant a chance to lead a role play, use all three case studies.
     - This will add approximately thirty minutes per case study, ninety minutes overall.
     - The ideal number of participants per group is three. This allows each person to play the role of leader. If there are more than three people in a group, they can repeat one of the case studies in order to practice the behaviors.
   - Have participants select who will be the Leader in Case Study 1, 2, and 3. As each case study begins, non-leaders will role play

the other characters in the scenario. For example, in Case Study 1, there will be a leader, a participant playing the role of Jeremy, and a participant playing Heather. If there are more participants than roles, ask the remaining people to observe and take notes.

- Using the notes they have taken about which leadership behaviors they'd use and how, the leader will address the other characters regarding the issue. Allow approximately five minutes for the leader to write a few bullet points for how he/she would approach the issue.
- Create the following flip chart to provide direction:

---

1. Form groups of three people.

2. Choose Leaders:
   - Role Play 1 (Case Study 1): _____
   - Role Play 2 (Case Study 2): _____
   - Role Play 3 (Case Study 3): _____

3. Leaders all spend five minutes, bullet points on what you will say

4. Role Play 1: Who will be Jeremy, Heather? Observer?

5. Conduct the role play: ten minutes

6. Give feedback: ten minutes

7. Switch to next role play: switch leaders, characters

- Conduct the role play and allow time for feedback to the leaders about how well they used the leadership behaviors.
- Debrief by asking the following questions:
  - *What did you learn about using the leadership behaviors?*
  - *What was difficult about the role play?*
  - *What did you see as observers or other characters when roles were played effectively by the leaders?*
  - *As leaders, what do you think you could have done better?*

- *How will this impact the way that you use the leadership behaviors in your daily work?*

COACH'S NOTES

If you are working one-on-one with a leader, you can adapt this activity in one of these two ways:

1. **Case Studies:** Rather than dealing all the cards out, you may choose to use only half of the deck, splitting the cards between you. Each of you then selects two or three behaviors that would apply to each case study and you determine the approach to the situation together, focusing on one case study per meeting.

2. **Role Plays:** After determining an approach to the case study, discuss the steps that the leader would take to implement the action plan. Ask what the leader would do, how he/she would do it, and what he/she would say, following the role-play instructions in the third variation above.

HANDOUT 3
LEADERSHIP
CASE STUDIES

CASE STUDY 1

Two team members, Jeremy and Heather, are not talking to each other—but they are talking about each other to everyone else. You are worried that their deteriorating relationship may begin to affect team performance and are considering how you will approach them with this issue.

1. What are the themes of this workplace challenge, issue, or situation?

    _____

    _____

    _____

    _____

2. Who is impacted as a result of the challenge, issue, or situation?

    _____

    _____

    _____

    _____

3. How does the challenge, issue, or situation affect relationships?

_____

_____

_____

_____

4. How does the challenge, issue, or situation affect organization/
   unit/team results?

_____

_____

_____

_____

5. Which LPI behaviors did you and your group select? What specific
   actions would you take to address this challenging situation with
   each behavior, and in what sequence? Create your action plan here:

   LPI # _____   _____

   LPI # _____   _____

   LPI # _____   _____

   LPI # _____   _____

   LPI # _____   _____

6. Which of the five leadership practices will be developed by addressing the situation this way?

___ Model the Way

___ Inspire a Shared Vision

___ Challenge the Process

___ Enable Others to Act

___ Encourage the Heart

7. What have you learned about applying the LPI behaviors?

_____

_____

_____

_____

8. What was valuable about exploring this scenario?

_____

_____

_____

_____

CASE STUDY 2

Due to across-the-board budget cuts, your area must "do more with less." You've just been told that you must cut your staff by 10 percent within two weeks, but that you will still need to meet a key deadline without the expected resources. This will be disturbing news to those immediately impacted, and it will be unsettling news to the remainder of the team.

1. What are the themes of this workplace challenge, issue, or situation?

_____

_____

2. Who is impacted as a result of the challenge, issue, or situation?

_____

_____

3. How does the challenge, issue, or situation affect relationships?

_____

_____

4. How does the challenge, issue, or situation affect organization/unit/team results?

_____

_____

5. Which LPI behaviors did you and your group select? What specific actions would you take to address this challenging situation with each behavior, and in what sequence? Create your action plan here:

LPI # ____ _____

LPI # ____ _____

LPI # ____ _____

LPI # ____ _____

LPI # ____ _____

6. Which of the five leadership practices will be developed by addressing the situation this way?
   ___ Model the Way
   ___ Inspire a Shared Vision
   ___ Challenge the Process
   ___ Enable Others to Act
   ___ Encourage the Heart

7. What have you learned about applying the LPI behaviors?

_____

_____

8. What was valuable about exploring this scenario?

_____

_____

CASE STUDY 3

You and two members of a major project team agreed on a plan for the project you are all working on. You just overheard that one of members has taken an entirely different approach that can impact the work you are doing. This type of communication problem between you and the other person has happened before, and this time it will cause serious delays in completing this major project.

1. What are the themes of this workplace challenge, issue, or situation?

_____

_____

_____

_____

2. Who is impacted as a result of the challenge, issue, or situation?

_____

_____

_____

_____

3. How does the challenge, issue, or situation affect relationships?

_____

_____

_____

4. How does the challenge, issue, or situation affect organization/ unit/team results?

_____

_____

_____

5. Which LPI behaviors did you and your group select? What specific actions would you take to address this challenging situation with each behavior, and in what sequence? Create your action plan here:

LPI # _____ _____

LPI # _____ _____

LPI # _____ _____

LPI # _____ _____

LPI # _____ _____

6. Which of the five leadership practices will be developed by addressing the situation this way?

____ Model the Way

____ Inspire a Shared Vision

____ Challenge the Process

____ Enable Others to Act

____ Encourage the Heart

7. What have you learned about applying the LPI behaviors?

_____

_____

_____

8. What was valuable about exploring this scenario?

_____

_____

_____

HANDOUT 4
OUR REAL WORK SITUATIONS AND LPI BEHAVIORS APPLICATION

Directions: This is a tool you can use to apply the LPI behaviors to your real-life leadership challenges, issues, and situations. Use this handout as a reflection tool for yourself—and to share with your work team, peers, and manager to tackle different issues as they arise.

Briefly describe your team/unit/organization challenge, issue, and situation:

Ask these questions:

1. What are the themes of this challenge, issue, or situation?

2. Who is impacted as a result of the challenge, issue, or situation?

3. How does the challenge, issue, or situation affect relationships?

4. How does the challenge, issue, or situation affect organization/ unit/team results?

Leadership Practices Inventory (LPI) Action Cards
Copyright © 2010 by James M. Kouzes and Barry Z. Posner.
Reproduced by permission of Pfeiffer, an Imprint of Wiley. www.pfeiffer.com.

Directions: Use the following format for creating an action plan to address each challenge, issue, or situation:

1. Which four or five LPI behaviors would be critical to address/resolve the situation and to create an action plan?

    LPI # _____ _____

    LPI # _____ _____

    LPI # _____ _____

    LPI # _____ _____

    LPI # _____ _____

2. Which of the five leadership practices will be developed by addressing the situation this way?

    ____ Model the Way

    ____ Inspire a Shared Vision

    ____ Challenge the Process

    ____ Enable Others to Act

    ____ Encourage the Heart

3. What have you learned about applying the LPI behaviors?

    _____

    _____

    _____

ACTIVITY 4
YOUR CHALLENGING
LEADERSHIP SITUATION

ACTIVITY OVERVIEW

In this activity, participants use the LPI Action Cards to help them assess and resolve a leadership dilemma.

PURPOSE

Help participants learn the *Leadership Practices Inventory* behaviors and use them in real work situations to be a more effective leaders. Participants will be able to:

- Use the thirty LPI behaviors to apply specific actions to workplace issues when they need to see improved results
- Use LPI Action Cards on their own and with their teams or others for future workplace issue resolution
- Use the LPI behaviors to solicit recommendations from their peers regarding suggestions for resolving a workplace issue
- Create action plans for on-the-job commitment to the workplace issue resolution with commitment partners

PARTICIPANTS

Minimum: 3
Maximum: None
Recommended: 12 to 15
   (Participants work in groups of three to five in this activity.)

PREREQUISITE

Familiarity with LPI behaviors. Suggested pre-work includes the Introductory Activities (Activities 1 and 2) included in this

Facilitator's Guide, as well as the LPI Action Card Case Studies activity (Activity 3). Completion of the *Leadership Practices Inventory* is highly recommended.

TIME

1 hour and 15 minutes, which includes setup, the activity, and the debriefing

SUPPLIES AND RESOURCES

- LPI Action Card deck for each group
- LPI Action Card deck for each participant to take away
- Your Challenging Leadership Situation handout (number 5) for each participant
- The Thirty Leadership Behaviors handout (number 2) or, if participants have taken the LPI:
  - LPI Survey Reports, turned to the Leadership Behaviors Ranking page

Note: before this activity, have the LPI Action Cards and handouts ready to provide to participants.

FACILITATOR NOTES

Activity Setup

- Divide participants into table groups of three to five. Ask them to sit at their tables so they can play a game, with the table clear of materials and other workshop items.
- Distribute one deck of LPI Action Cards to each table group.
- Distribute the Your Challenging Leadership Situation handout (number 5) to all participants.

Overview

The LPI leadership behaviors provide a rich starting point for leadership development. Whether or not participants have completed the LPI, they can use the LPI leadership behaviors to focus their development. Applying the behaviors to real-life situations deepens one's understanding of the behaviors and how they can influence positive outcomes for leaders and those around them.

In this activity, participants apply the *Leadership Practices Inventory* behaviors to workplace issues of their own. As a result, they should be able to use the thirty LPI behaviors to apply specific actions to workplace issues when they need to see improved results, both on their own and with their team or with others. Participants will solicit recommendations from their peers regarding suggestions for resolving the issue using the LPI behaviors and create action plans for on-the-job commitment to the workplace issue resolution with commitment partners.

Leaders should apply these behaviors to their work on projects, to improve performance and quality, and to help meet their goals and targets. These behaviors can be applied to ANY workplace issue a leader experiences.

Participants will work in small groups to play a card game for which the object is to use a selection of the thirty LPI behaviors to resolve specific leadership challenges participants are currently facing, for example, issues with peers, their managers, other departments, customers, direct reports, productivity, and so forth. Through the activity, they will learn more about applying some of the LPI behaviors to real-life, unresolved, challenging leadership situations that are impacting their ability to achieve team/unit/organization results.

Introduce the Activity

Have participants open their LPI Report to the Leadership Behaviors Ranking page or use The Thirty Leadership Behaviors handout.

Have participants independently complete questions 1 and 2 on the Your Challenging Leadership Situation handout (allow six to eight minutes for reflection). They are to:

- Briefly describe the situation, including the primary challenges and who is involved.
- Explain how this situation affects results and why these results are important.

Next they will have an opportunity to share their situations with their table groups and get some help addressing them using the LPI behaviors through a fun and meaningful activity.

Play the Game

For the first round, provide the following instructions one step at a time to get the groups accustomed to the process they will use for the activity. Afterward, they will cycle through the rounds on their own.

- *Step 1:* Have a person at each table volunteer to go first and share his/her challenging business situation as described on his/her Your Challenging Leadership Situation handout. (Allow up to two minutes for each person to describe a situation to the table group.)
- *Step 2:* Each team selects a dealer. The dealer shuffles the cards and deals them out to everyone in the table group, dealing out all the cards in the deck. Some individuals may have more cards than others. (Step 2 takes about one minute.)
- *Step 3:* Each person reviews his/her "hand." Notice that each card has three identifications: the number of the LPI behavior, one of the five leadership practices, and the specific LPI behavior that relates to the number. Each participant mentally selects the BEST behavior to help address the situation/problem. (Step 3 takes three to four minutes.)
- *Step 4:* Starting with the person to the left of the participant with the challenging situation, each person takes a turn placing the selected LPI Action Card in the center of the table. Each participant reads the LPI number and the LPI behavior aloud and explains how this behavior can address the

situation. All cards should then be placed in front of the person who has the situation. This person also chooses an LPI Action Card from his or her own "hand" and places it next to the others. (Step 4 takes six to eight minutes.)

- *Step 5:* Once the group is finished, have the person who owns the leadership issue make notes on his/her Your Challenging Leadership Situation handout with his/her own LPI behavior as well as those of the other players. Often there are one or two behaviors that are most applicable as first steps to resolving the issue. Allow four minutes for the completion of the question on the Your Challenging Situation handout and for the individual to quickly review his/her LPI Report to see where these are ranked on the report (if applicable). Ask:
  - Which LPI behaviors did you and your group identify to address this challenging situation?

Complete the Activity

Have the table groups start Round 2 and repeat Steps 1 through 5; afterward continue with rounds until all the table groups have completed Steps 1 through 5 for each participant's situation.

At the end of all the rounds, participants will answer the final two questions on the Action Plan of the Your Challenging Leadership Situation handout, considering the LPI behavior actions they will take with their respective business issues. If participants have taken the LPI survey, they will focus on their answers in the action plans on their LPI reports, identifying where the LPI behaviors ranked on their reports and analyzing their strengths and opportunities for growth. Allow eight to ten minutes. They should fill in the following information:

- People with whom you will follow up for this action plan
- Your name
- Your commitment partner (chosen in this session or in a previous session)

- Today's date
- Date for implementing action plan and following up with commitment partner

Debrief

Ask participants the following questions, and probe for more information when necessary:

- *What was valuable about sharing your leadership situation with others?*

    (Possible responses: hearing another perspective, additional ideas that I may not have thought of on my own)

- *What was valuable about hearing about someone else's situation?*

    (Possible responses: helps us to see that others are also experiencing similar challenges)

- *What are some examples of how you will apply the LPI behaviors to your business situations?*

    (Possible responses: specific behaviors will be practiced)

- *What difference do you anticipate using the LPI behaviors will make in your situations?*

    (Possible responses: because it will involve taking a different approach than I normally do; it will stretch me, as well as those involved)

- *What LPI behaviors will you be developing?*

    (Possible responses: specific behaviors)

- *What leadership practices will you be developing?*

    (Possible responses: specific practices)

- *What have we learned about applying the LPI behaviors?*

    (Possible responses: If you can apply them to an actual situation, you can build skills as well as resolving a business challenge.)

Wrap Up

This same activity can be re-created over and over, applying it to new challenging business situations.

Encourage participants to share this activity with their work teams to tackle challenges as they arise using the LPI behaviors as solutions. Share with participants:

- *This is an exercise that you can do on your own or with another group when you have a challenging business or leadership situation that you are facing.*
- *It will help you not only practice the behaviors, but will help you be mindful of your actions and help to get better results.*

Thank the group for their participation.

Distribute one LPI Action Card deck per participant if they do not yet have their own decks.

VARIATIONS

1. **Three Meetings:** If short amounts of time are available over a period, participants can focus on one real workplace issue per meeting. This allows reinforcement of the leadership behaviors over time as well as practice using the cards. It creates a "coaching circle" wherein leaders coach and are coached by each other.

2. **Take a Different Perspective:** Participants take one of several perspectives based on the leader's challenge. This deepens the analysis of the situations. (*Note:* The depth of discussion in this option may require adding time to the activity.)
   - This variation works best in groups of three.
   - Depending on the leader's challenge, participants may take one of the following perspectives in analyzing the issue (leaders would add those that are appropriate to their own situations):

- Manager
- Peer
- Human Resources Director
- Direct Report
- Customer (Internal or External)

- From this perspective they choose the LPI Action Cards they think most appropriate. For example, if the leader is experiencing a challenge with a direct report, one participant may take the perspective of a direct report and choose number 14 from his/her hand, "Treats people with dignity and respect" rather than number 8, "Challenges people to take new approaches," because the direct report is looking at the problem from his/her own perspective and may dislike change in that particular situation.

- Debrief the activity by asking those who took each perspective to report out on how they viewed the challenge differently. They can also provide coaching to the leader. Ask:
  - *How did your perspective impact the leadership behaviors that you chose?*
  - *In what kinds of situations may you want to take on these different perspectives in order to analyze an issue?* (Bonus! What behavior does this represent? Number 9, "Actively listens to diverse points of view.")
  - *What coaching did you have for the leader based on your perspective?*

3. **Role Play:** Allowing leaders to role play using the leadership behaviors provides a way for leaders to practice in a controlled environment. Speaking the words they would use in their situation challenges leaders, prepares them to address the situation, and provides a great learning opportunity. To create a role play at the end of a leader's challenge, utilize the roles demonstrated in Variation 2, adding roles if necessary and follow the steps below.
  - Logistics:

- The ideal number of participants per group is three. This allows each person to play the role of leader.
- This will add approximately thirty minutes per leader or ninety minutes overall.
- Have participants select who will go first, second, and third in leading their own role plays. As each role play begins, non-leaders will play the other characters in the scenario based on the instruction by the leader. For example, in role play 1, there will be a leader and participants playing two roles chosen by the leader (perhaps two direct reports or a colleague and an observer). If there are more participants than roles, ask the remaining people to observe and take notes.
- Using the notes they have taken about which leadership behaviors they'd use and how, the leaders will address the other characters regarding the issue. Allow approximately five minutes for the leaders to write a few bullet points for how they would approach the issue.
- Create the following flip chart to provide direction:

---

1. Get into groups of three people.
2. Choose leaders:
   - Role Play 1 (Leader 1): _____
   - Role Play 2 (Leader 2): _____
   - Role Play 3 (Leader 3): _____
3. Leaders all spend five minutes; list bullet points on what you will say.
4. Role Play 1: What are the roles and who will play them? Observer?
5. Conduct the role play: ten minutes.
6. Give feedback: ten minutes.
7. Switch to next role play: switch leaders, characters

- Conduct the role play and allow time for feedback to the leaders about how well they used the appropriate leadership behaviors.
- Debrief by asking the following questions:
  - *What did you learn about using the leadership behaviors?*
  - *What was difficult about the role play?*
  - *What did you see as observers or other characters that was done effectively by the leaders?*
  - *As leaders, what did you think you could have done better?*
  - *How will what you have learned help you with the situation you addressed?*
  - *How will this role-play activity impact the way that you use the leadership behaviors in your daily work?*

COACH'S NOTES

If you are working one-on-one with a leader, you can adapt this activity in other ways, for example:

1. **Discuss the Challenging Leadership Situation:** This is an excellent way to help leaders apply the leadership behaviors to daily situations. Rather than dealing all the cards out, you may choose to use only half of the deck, splitting the cards between you. Each of you then selects two or three behaviors that would apply to the workplace situation and together you determine the approach to the situation, focusing on one business situation per meeting.

2. **Role Plays:** After determining an approach to the situation, discuss the steps that the leader would take to implement the action plan. Ask what the leader would do, how he/she would do it, and what he/she would say, following the role-play instructions in Variation 4 above.

HANDOUT 2
THE THIRTY LEADERSHIP BEHAVIORS

The Five Practices of Exemplary Leadership	The Thirty Leadership Behaviors
Model the Way	1. Sets a personal example of what he/she expects of others.
	6. Makes certain that people adhere to agreed-on standards.
	11. Follows through on promises and commitments.
	16. Asks for feedback for how his/her actions affect people's performance.
	21. Builds consensus around organization's values.
	26. Is clear about his/her philosophy of leadership.
Inspire a Shared Vision	2. Talks about future trends influencing our work.
	7. Describes a compelling image of the future.
	12. Appeals to others to share dream of the future.
	17. Shows others how their interests can be realized.
	22. Paints "big picture" of group aspirations.
	27. Speaks with conviction about the meaning of work.

(Continued)

The Five Practices of Exemplary Leadership	The Thirty Leadership Behaviors
Challenge the Process	3. Seeks challenging opportunities to test skills.
	8. Challenges people to try new approaches.
	13. Searches outside organization for innovative ways to improve.
	18. Asks "What can we learn?"
	23. Makes certain that goals, plans, and milestones are set.
	28. Experiments and takes risks.
Enable Others to Act	4. Develops cooperative relationships.
	9. Actively listens to diverse points of view.
	14. Treats people with dignity and respect.
	19. Supports decisions other people make.
	24. Gives people choice about how to do their work.
	29. Ensures that people grow in their jobs.
Encourage the Heart	5. Praises people for a job well done.
	10. Expresses confidence in people's abilities.
	15. Creatively rewards people for their contributions.
	20. Recognizes people for commitment to shared values.
	25. Finds ways to celebrate accomplishments.
	30. Gives team members appreciation and support.

HANDOUT 5
YOUR CHALLENGING
SITUATION

Directions: Consider the leadership challenges you are facing, and then identify a specific situation for which you need to see improved results. The situation should be presently unresolved.

Briefly describe the situation, including the primary challenges and who is involved:

_____

_____

_____

_____

How does the challenge, issue, or situation affect organization/unit/team results?

_____

_____

_____

_____

ACTION PLAN

Directions: Use the following for creating an action plan to address each challenge, issue, or situation:

1. Which four or five LPI behaviors would be critical to address/resolve the situation and to create an action plan?

    LPI # _____ _____

    LPI # _____ _____

    LPI # _____ _____

    LPI # _____ _____

    LPI # _____ _____

2. What will you do differently to address this situation?

    _____

    _____

3. People with whom you will follow up for this action plan:

    _____

    _____

4. Your Commitment
    Your Name: _____
    Your Commitment Partner: _____
    Today's Date: _____
    Date for Implementing Your Action Plan: _____

ACTIVITY 5
LPI ACTION CARD SHUFFLE

ACTIVITY OVERVIEW

In this activity, participants continue to focus on the *Leadership Practices Inventory* (LPI) behaviors, making them a part of their everyday leadership practice.

PURPOSE

Help participants address leadership behaviors on a regular basis by practicing a behavior selected in the LPI Action Card Shuffle. Participants will be able to:

- Use the LPI Action Cards to direct their leadership development activities
- Assess and reflect on their leadership behaviors
- Develop improvement plans for their own leadership
- Coach other leaders and receive coaching on their leadership behaviors

PARTICIPANTS

Minimum: 1
Maximum: 40
Recommended: 12
   (Participants work on their own or in small groups in this activity.)

PREREQUISITE

Familiarity with LPI behaviors. Suggested pre-work includes one of the Introductory Activities such as "Leaders Tell Us . . . " and the LPI Action Card board game, as well as completion of the *Leadership Practices Inventory*.

TIME

20 to 45 minutes, including setup, the activity, and debriefing

SUPPLIES AND RESOURCES

- LPI Action Card deck for each participant for the individual activity
- LPI Action Card deck for each group for the group activity
- LPI Survey Report, turned to the Leadership Behaviors Ranking page (if participants have completed the survey)
- Card Shuffle Reflection Questions handout (number 6) for each participant
- Pen or pencil for each participant
- Journal or planner for each participant

FACILITATOR NOTES

Activity Setup
- For the group activity, divide participants into pairs or groups of three.
- Distribute the Card Shuffle Reflection Questions handout (number 6) to each participant.
- Distribute one deck of LPI Action Cards per table (or participant for the individual activity).

Overview
This is an activity that leaders can engage in to address leadership behaviors on a regular basis by practicing a behavior selected in the LPI Action Card Shuffle. Leadership is learned and doesn't just

come without practice and reflection. As Kouzes and Posner say, "There is no success without the possibility of failure . . . [leaders] ask "What can be learned from the experience?"

Through what they learn in the LPI Action Card Shuffle, participants will be able to use the LPI Action Cards to direct their leadership development activities, assessing and reflecting on their leadership behaviors and what they have learned. They will develop improvement plans for their own leadership, as well as coach other leaders and receive coaching on their leadership behaviors. Encourage leaders to set a schedule to do this activity each day or week.

Introduce the Activity

- Individual Activity: On a weekly or bi-weekly basis, leaders shuffle their LPI Action Card decks. They then select one behavior for focus for the given period (one or two weeks). Using a journal or planner, leaders develop ideas for improvement in this behavior. They should consider what they are doing well, what they can do better, and plan for their next opportunity to use this behavior. If they have completed the Leadership Practices Inventory, they should consider their LPI feedback (especially the page ranking the thirty behaviors) when doing the activity.
- Group Activity: In a group setting, you can set up pairs or groups of three to discuss these questions. Provide time up-front for each person to think through the questions on the handout and respond in writing. Then have them share their behavior with their group members and coach each other with additional ideas.

Complete the Activity

Provide a Card Shuffle Reflection Questions handout for each participant. The handout includes the following questions to consider:

1. If you have completed the Leadership Practices Inventory, where does the behavior fall in your LPI Behavior Ranking in your LPI report? What is the score? What is your goal regarding the behavior and the LPI? For example, would you like to raise the score or raise the behavior ranking, etc. (Note: If you have not completed the LPI, move to Question 2.)

2. What is a specific example of a time when you have done this behavior well?
   - What made you a success in this situation? Why?
   - Who was involved in this situation? Why?
   - What can you learn from this situation that you can apply to other situations? Why?

3. What is a specific example of a time when you were not successful in using this behavior well?
   - What made this situation challenging? Why?
   - Who was involved in this situation? Why?
   - What can you learn from this situation that you can apply to others? In what way?

4. Who might be a good resource to provide feedback on how you have used this behavior in the past?

5. Who might be a good coach for you on this behavior as you plan to use it in the future?

6. Refer to The Leadership Challenge, fourth edition, for the practice that this behavior belongs to. What insights do you have from your reading about this practice?

7. Describe a current business situation for which you need to utilize this behavior.

8. What action steps will you take in this situation to practice this leadership behavior? By when?
   - What barriers might you experience as you practice this leadership behavior?
   - What will you do to overcome these barriers?

Debrief

Ask participants the following questions, and probe for more information when necessary:

- *What are some examples of behaviors that you selected for development?*
- *What helpful advice or insights did you hear from your team members?*
- *What will you do to work on this behavior in the next week? When?*

Wrap Up

This is an activity that leaders should repeat frequently to address and practice their leadership behaviors. Participants should use the LPI Action Cards to direct their leadership development activities, assessing and reflecting on their leadership behaviors. As they develop improvement plans for their own leadership and coach other leaders and receive coaching on their leadership behaviors, the frequency and skill with which they lead will improve.

Encourage leaders to set a schedule to do this activity on a weekly or bi-weekly basis.

Share with participants:

- *Leadership is clearly learned. As you continue to practice, ask for feedback, and increase the frequency of your leadership behaviors, your leadership skill will continue to develop.*

Thank the group for their participation.

VARIATIONS

1. **Top Five, Bottom Ten:** Leaders use the LPI Action Card deck and their LPI ranking of thirty behaviors or The Thirty Leadership Behaviors handout (number 2) if they have not

completed the *Leadership Practices Inventory*. They search through the cards and pull out those that they believe are their top five behaviors and bottom ten behaviors. These fifteen behaviors can be the focus of their leadership efforts as they continue to learn and grow their skills.

- If participants have not completed the LPI, have them assess and label their top five and bottom ten behaviors on The Thirty Leadership Behaviors handout.
- *Top Five LPI Behaviors:* Leaders leverage strengths to help others succeed. Take a look at each of the strengths and ask the following questions (write observations in a journal or planner).
  - *What is a specific example of how you use this behavior well?*
  - *What made you a success in this situation? Why?*
  - *How and with whom can you leverage this success with others? (coaching? mentoring? etc.)*
- *Bottom Ten LPI Behaviors:* Just as a professional athlete focuses on improving his/her weakest areas with "practice, practice, practice," a professional leader should put most of his/her attention on developing those leadership behaviors that are ranked the lowest by others.
  - *Sort your bottom ten cards in order from lowest to highest. Choose one or two cards for focus for a specific period of time (say a week or number of weeks).*
  - *Ask the questions from the Card Shuffle Reflection Questions Handout, writing your observations in a journal or planner.*

2. **Gaps:** If leaders have completed the *Leadership Practices Inventory*, they can use the LPI Action Card deck and their LPI ranking of thirty behaviors to address those behaviors for which there is a significant gap between their perceptions and the perceptions of others (see the asterisks marking those behaviors on the Leadership Behaviors Ranking page). Have them search

through the cards and pull out those that correspond to the behaviors that have significant gaps. These behaviors can be the focus of their leadership efforts as they continue to learn and grow their skills. They should ask themselves the questions from the Card Shuffle Reflection Questions handout, writing their observations in a journal or planner.

COACH'S NOTES

If you are working one-on-one with a leader, you can adapt this activity. You may have the leader work through the individual activity first, and then debrief his/her answers and coach him/her on other approaches. You may also work together with the leader as outlined in the "Group Activity" above regarding working in pairs. Provide time up-front for the leader to think through these questions and respond in writing. Then discuss the answers and work with the leader to develop the actions he/she will take.

HANDOUT 6
CARD SHUFFLE REFLECTION
QUESTIONS

There is no success without the possibility of failure.

—*Jim Kouzes and Barry Posner*

Directions: Consider the following questions and write down your reflections in a journal, notebook, or planner. Writing down your reflections in a central location is an important part to developing a plan for the leadership skills you want to develop further; therefore this list of questions acts as a guide, rather than a location for you to write.

1. If you have completed the *Leadership Practices Inventory,* where does the behavior fall in your LPI Behavior Ranking in your LPI report? What is the score? What is your goal regarding the behavior and the LPI (raise the score to ___; or raise behavior to top 10, etc.)

2. What is a specific example of a time when you have done this behavior well?

    a. What made you a success in this situation? Why?

    b. Who was involved in this situation? Why?

    c. What can you learn from this situation that you can apply to others? Why?

3. What is a specific example of a time when you were *not* successful in using this behavior well?

    a. What made this situation challenging? Why?

    b. Who was involved in this situation? Why?

    c. What can you learn from this situation that you can apply to others? Why?

4. Who might be a good resource to provide feedback on how you have used this behavior in the past?

5. Who might be a good coach for you on this behavior as you plan to use it in the future?

6. Refer to *The Leadership Challenge* (4th ed.) for the practice that this behavior belongs to. What insights do you get from your reading on this practice?

7. Describe a current business situation for which you need to utilize this behavior.

8. What action steps will you take in this situation to practice this leadership behavior? By when?

   a. What barriers might you experience as you practice this leadership behavior?

   b. What will you do to overcome these barriers?

ACTIVITY 6
ALIGNING ACTIONS WITH
LEADERSHIP BEHAVIOR*

ACTIVITY OVERVIEW

In this activity, participants plan actions that will help them focus on the development of their LPI behaviors.

PURPOSE

Provide the opportunity for participants to determine specific actions they can take to practice their LPI behaviors. As a result of this activity, participants will be able to:

- Create action plans for developing key leadership behaviors further
- Take specific actions to practice leadership behaviors
- Work with commitment partners for ongoing development and accountability

PARTICIPANTS

Minimum: 1
Maximum: 40
Recommended: 12 to 15
   (Participants work on their own or in groups of four or five people for this activity.)

---

*Adapted from The Leadership Challenge Workshop (3rd ed.).

PREREQUISITE

LPI Action Card Shuffle (Activity 5), Variation "Top Five, Bottom Ten"

TIME

30 to 40 minutes for group activity; 60 minutes if individual activity is added

SUPPLIES AND RESOURCES

- The Thirty Leadership Behaviors handout (number 2) with Top Five, Bottom Ten identified from LPI Action Card Shuffle (Activity 5), Variation "Top Five, Bottom Ten" or
- LPI Survey Report, turned to the Leadership Behaviors Ranking page (if participants have completed the survey)
- Align Action with Leadership Behaviors handout (number 7) for each participant
- LPI Action Card Decks (one per participant)
- Flip-chart paper, easel, and markers for each group

FACILITATOR NOTES

Activity Setup

- Divide participants into table groups of four or five. Explain that participants will work in small groups to identify actions they can take to model their leadership behaviors.
- For this activity, each group will need access to an easel with flip-chart paper and markers.

Overview

The LPI leadership behaviors provide a rich starting point for leadership development. Whether or not participants have completed the Leadership Practices Inventory, they can use the LPI leadership behaviors to focus their development. Sometimes, however, it is difficult to determine what kinds of actions can impact the development of a particular behavior.

In this activity, participants plan actions that will help them focus on the development of their LPI behaviors. The activity provides the opportunity for participants to determine specific actions they can take to practice those behaviors. After the activity, participants will be able to create action plans for developing key leadership behaviors further and take specific actions to practice them. Commitment partners will help leaders hold themselves and others accountable for the actions they create.

Introduce the Activity

Share with participants that there are many ways that they can take specific, visible actions to model their leadership behaviors.

For example, if a leader's value is "teamwork," you would see that leader demonstrate the value if he/she ensures that the team meets to discuss critical issues or if he/she encourages team members to seek out others to gain additional input. Another example is "honesty." If a leader has a value of honesty, he/she provides information and shares (within reason) his/her thoughts. For example, a leader may say, "I'll tell you what I know, find out, or let you know that I have information but cannot share it" in order to be as transparent as possible.

Ask participants for other examples of things leaders can do to demonstrate their leadership behaviors. Elicit a few responses and write them on the flip-chart page.

Share that there is a tool to help leaders determine what actions can help them focus on the leadership behaviors.

Briefly review each of the six ways in which leaders demonstrate leadership behaviors. They are

- Calendars
- Critical Incidents

- Stories
- Language
- Measurements
- Rewards

Hand out the Align Actions with Leadership Behaviors worksheet.

Ask participants to take a couple of minutes to read each of the descriptions on the worksheet. Then briefly explain some of the categories. For example:

- *Calendars: You need to be aware of how you spend your time. If you say your leadership behavior is developing your people, and you want to improve LPI behavior number 29, "Ensures that people grow in their jobs." How much time do you actually spend talking with individuals about their progress and development needs as opposed to focusing on other tasks?*

- *Stories: Ever hear people say, "And the moral of the story is . . . ?" Stories are colorful ways to talk about leadership behaviors. If you are working on LPI behavior 8, "Challenges people to try new approaches," tell a story about how an employee stopped the assembly line because defective products were being produced, fixed the problem, and enabled the company to retain its record of near-perfect quality.*

- *Rewards: To what extent do you recognize and reward people for upholding the leadership behaviors you believe in? "Rewards" is all about LPI behavior 20, "Recognizing people for commitment to shared leadership behaviors." Do you only recognize people for financial results or do you reward them for things like being collaborative with colleagues or honest with customers in tough situations? In other words, for practicing the leadership behaviors that you say are important?*

If you are working to develop Encourage the Heart, what rewards can you give that are personalized and creative?

- *Measurement: Measuring how others live a specific leadership behavior sounds difficult, right? How do you measure 'honesty,' for example. There are ways to set informal, and formal, measurements. If you are working on LPI behavior 4, "Develops cooperative relationships," you can assess how often you work together on a project, versus working alone. When you challenge yourself to come up with measurements for your leadership behaviors, you will have valuable feedback on how your actions are aligned.*

Ask participants to turn to the sample in the worksheet. Quickly review the sample.

First complete the group activity to demonstrate how to use the worksheet. Then allow participants to complete the worksheet with a leadership behavior that is specific to their own development.

Group Activity

Form small groups (four to five people).

1. Ask each group to select a leadership behavior one of the group members identified during the "Top Five, Bottom Ten" variation of the LPI Action Card Shuffle (Activity 5).
2. Give the groups three to five minutes to brainstorm some actions they can take to model the leadership behavior they selected, using the categories listed on their worksheets. These may be actions that are currently being done, suggestions or new ideas, or current activities that should be stopped. Explain that they do not have to have responses

for every category, and that they can add a new category if they wish.

3. Ask participants to record their responses from the Align Actions with Leadership Behaviors worksheet onto a flip-chart page. (There is no need to re-create the chart in whole; simply have participants write the category and one or two bullet points for their answers.)

4. When time is up, ask groups to post their flip-chart pages where the entire group can see them. Ask everyone to walk around the room and review the posted responses. Suggest that participants write down any of the other groups' suggestions that appeal to them, asking for clarification if needed.

Remind participants that the purpose of the previous activity was to get them thinking about how to connect actions with leadership behaviors. Explain that you will now give them a few minutes to select a leadership behavior that they would like to develop further, reflect on it, and identify some ways they can practice the leadership behavior more frequently.

Individual Activity

Ask participants to turn to the other blank worksheet. Give them four to five minutes to do the following:

1. Select a leadership behavior that they would like to develop, preferably a different leadership behavior than the one they worked on in small groups. Write the leadership behavior at the top of the handout.

2. Complete the handout by indicating what they can do in the different categories to model and practice that leadership

behavior. They do not have to have responses for each category, and they can add a new category if they wish.
3. When they have completed their worksheets, ask participants to find commitment partners with whom they can share their responses and gain additional suggestions. Have them arrange times with their commitment partners to follow up with each other on how they are doing.

Debrief
Ask participants the following questions, and probe for more information when necessary:

- *How easy is it to come up with actions to demonstrate the leadership behaviors?*
  - (Possible responses: There are a lot of things people can do; the hard part is following through on those actions consistently; you cannot do one action a week and expect people to view you differently, etc.)
- *What will it take for you to ensure that you follow through and act in ways consistent with your shared leadership behaviors?*
  - (Possible responses: Schedule these actions into your week; set aside time in staff meetings for recognition or to institute "moments of truth"; great examples of someone on the team demonstrating a leadership behavior, etc.)

Wrap Up
Have participants share some of their ideas with one another.

Thank the group for their participation.

VARIATIONS

1. **Saving Time:** If you are short on time, you can skip Step 4 of the Group Activity or have individuals work on their own rather than in a group (see Individual Activity instructions). Then ask each group (or individual) to share one or two examples of the leadership behavior they selected and the responses they wrote on the worksheet.

2. **Role Play:** Allowing leaders to role play using the leadership behaviors provides a way for leaders to practice in a controlled environment. Speaking the words they would use to align the leadership behaviors they chose prepares them to demonstrate the behavior and provides a great learning opportunity. To create a role play, follow the steps below.
   - Logistics:
     - The ideal number of participants per group is three. This allows each person to play the role of leader.
     - This will add approximately thirty minutes per leader or ninety minutes overall.
   - Have participants select who will go first, second, and third in leading their own role plays. As each role play begins, non-leaders will play the other characters in the scenario based on the instruction by the leader. For example, in role play 1, there will be a leader and participants playing two roles chosen by the leader (perhaps two direct reports or a colleague and an observer). If there are more participants than roles, ask the remaining people to observe and take notes.
   - Using the notes they have taken about which leadership behaviors they'd use and how, the leader will address the other characters regarding the issue. Allow approximately five minutes for the leaders to write a few bullet points for how they would approach the issue.
   - Create the following flip chart to provide direction:

1. Get into groups of three people.
2. Choose leaders:
    *   Role Play 1 (Leader 1): _____
    *   Role Play 2 (Leader 2): _____
    *   Role Play 3 (Leader 3): _____
3. Leaders all spend five minutes; list bullet points on what you will say.
4. Role Play 1: What are the roles and who will play them? Observer?
5. Conduct the role play: ten minutes.
6. Give feedback: ten minutes.
7. Switch to next role play: switch leaders, characters

*   Conduct the role play and allow time for feedback to the leaders about how well they used the appropriate leadership behaviors.
*   Debrief by asking the following questions:
    *   *What did you learn about using the leadership behaviors?*
    *   *What was difficult about the role play?*
    *   *What did you see as observers or other characters that was done effectively by the leaders?*
    *   *As leaders, what did you think you could have done better?*
    *   *How will what you have learned help you with the situation you addressed?*
    *   *How will this role-play activity impact the way that you use the leadership behaviors in your daily work?*

COACH'S NOTES

If you are working one-on-one with a leader, you can adapt this activity. First, work together with the leader to complete the Group Activity by determining several actions you can take to align activities around one leadership behavior, perhaps a behavior that is important in the organization or a general leadership behavior that many share. This will generate ideas that can be applied to another important leadership behavior that the leader would like to demonstrate in his or her leadership. Once you've completed the Group Activity, the leader may complete the Individual Activity on his/her own. Debrief the activity together, suggesting additional ways that the leaders could demonstrate the leadership behavior as needed.

You may also conduct the role play with the leader, providing coaching and developing an approach on how to apply the leadership behaviors more consistently.

HANDOUT 2
THE THIRTY LEADERSHIP BEHAVIORS

The Five Practices of Exemplary Leadership	The Thirty Leadership Behaviors
Model the Way	1. Sets a personal example of what he/she expects of others. 6. Makes certain that people adhere to agreed-on standards. 11. Follows through on promises and commitments. 16. Asks for feedback for how his/her actions affect people's performance. 21. Builds consensus around organization's values. 26. Is clear about his/her philosophy of leadership.
Inspire a Shared Vision	2. Talks about future trends influencing our work. 7. Describes a compelling image of the future. 12. Appeals to others to share dream of the future. 17. Shows others how their interests can be realized. 22. Paints "big picture" of group aspirations. 27. Speaks with conviction about the meaning of work.

(Continued)

The Five Practices of Exemplary Leadership	The Thirty Leadership Behaviors
Challenge the Process	3. Seeks challenging opportunities to test skills.
	8. Challenges people to try new approaches.
	13. Searches outside organization for innovative ways to improve.
	18. Asks "What can we learn?"
	23. Makes certain that goals, plans, and milestones are set.
	28. Experiments and takes risks.
Enable Others to Act	4. Develops cooperative relationships.
	9. Actively listens to diverse points of view.
	14. Treats people with dignity and respect.
	19. Supports decisions other people make.
	24. Gives people choice about how to do their work.
	29. Ensures that people grow in their jobs.
Encourage the Heart	5. Praises people for a job well done.
	10. Expresses confidence in people's abilities.
	15. Creatively rewards people for their contributions.
	20. Recognizes people for commitment to shared values.
	25. Finds ways to celebrate accomplishments.
	30. Gives team members appreciation and support.

HANDOUT 7
ALIGN ACTIONS WITH LEADERSHIP BEHAVIORS

Calendar

Leaders need to be aware of how they spend their time. If you say you use leadership behavior developing your people, and you want to improve LPI behavior 29, "Ensures that people grow in their jobs," how much time do you actually spend talking with individuals about their progress and development needs, as opposed to focusing on other tasks?

Critical Incidents

These significant moments of learning and are often referred to as "teachable moments." Are you using unexpected occurrences to demonstrate appropriate leadership behaviors? In the case of a product recall, are you demonstrating the importance of good customer service by proactively contacting your customers and asking "What can we learn?" or are you spending time determining the effect this will have on future revenue?

Stories

Ever hear people say, "And the moral of the story is . . . ?" Stories are colorful ways to talk about leadership behaviors. If you are working on LPI behavior 8, "Challenges people to try new approaches," tell a story about how an employee stopped the assembly line because defective products were being produced, fixed the problem, and enabled the company to retain its record of near-perfect quality.

Language

Leaders understand the power of words, and they often choose them carefully. Metaphors and analogies can be effective for creating a vision, and the questions leaders ask often frame the issues and set the agenda. How does your choice of words illustrate leadership behaviors?

Measurements

Measuring how others live a specific leadership behavior sounds difficult, right? How do you measure Honesty, for example. There are ways to set informal, and formal, measurements. If you are working on LPI behavior 4, "Develops cooperative relationships," you can assess how often you are working together on a project, versus working alone. When you challenge yourself to come up with measurements for your leadership behaviors, you will have valuable feedback on how your actions are aligned to your goals.

Rewards

To what extent do you recognize and reward people for upholding the leadership behaviors you believe in? LPI behavior 20, "Recognizing people for commitment to shared leadership behaviors," is all about rewards. Do you only recognize people for financial results, or do you reward them for things like being collaborative with colleagues or honest with customers in tough situations? In other words, for practicing the leadership behaviors that you say are important? If you are working to develop Encourage the Heart, what rewards can you give that are personalized and creative?

SAMPLE HANDOUT 7
ALIGN ACTIONS WITH
LEADERSHIP BEHAVIORS

Behavior 16: Ask for feedback for how my actions affect people's performance

Action Ideas

Calendar

Schedule time at the end of each quarter to review my performance and ask for feedback from the team.

    After each project milestone, ask the team for feedback on steps we can take in the future to increase the potential for success.

Critical Incidents

The next time we fall behind and it appears we will not make a milestone deadline, ask for immediate input from the team on what steps I can take to get the project back on track.

Stories

Use a story from my past experience to encourage my direct reports to provide honest and critical feedback on my performance.

Language

I will be sure to thank the individual for providing feedback to me, even if I am not in agreement.

Measurements

Include 360-degree feedback as part of my annual review. Set tangible goals as a result of that feedback.

Use the LPI annually to help me focus on and improve critical leadership behaviors. Compare current ratings to those of the previous year.

Rewards

During status meetings recognize team members who provided feedback that directly improved performance.

HANDOUT 7
ALIGN ACTIONS WITH
LEADERSHIP BEHAVIORS

Behavior #: _____   Behavior: _____

Action Ideas

Calendar

_____

_____

_____

_____

Critical Incidents

_____

_____

_____

_____

Stories

_____

_____

_____

_____

Leadership Practices Inventory (LPI) Action Cards
Copyright © 2010 by James M. Kouzes and Barry Z. Posner.
Reproduced by permission of Pfeiffer, an Imprint of Wiley. www.pfeiffer.com.

Language

_____

_____

_____

_____

Measurements

_____

_____

_____

_____

Rewards

_____

_____

_____

_____

HANDOUT 7
ALIGN ACTIONS WITH
LEADERSHIP BEHAVIORS

Behavior #: _____   Behavior: _____

Action Ideas

Calendar

_____

_____

_____

_____

Critical Incidents

_____

_____

_____

Stories

_____

_____

_____

_____

Language

_____

_____

_____

_____

Measurements

_____

_____

_____

Rewards

_____

_____

_____

REINFORCEMENT ACTIVITIES

Activity 7: Barriers and Tactics

Activity 8: Leadership Behavior Combinations

Activity 9: Feedback and Coaching Circle

ACTIVITY 7
BARRIERS AND TACTICS

ACTIVITY OVERVIEW

In this activity, participants identify barriers to utilizing leadership behaviors and develop tactics to overcome those barriers.

PURPOSE

The purpose of this activity is to provide an opportunity for leaders to determine barriers to their leadership development and to create tactics that will help them address and overcome those barriers. As a result of this activity, participants will be able to:

- Identify barriers to utilizing the leadership behaviors
- Develop tactics that address barriers to developing their leadership

PARTICIPANTS

Minimum: 3
Maximum: 30
Recommended: 15
   (Participants work in groups of three to five in this activity.)

PREREQUISITE

LPI Action Card Shuffle (Activity 5), Variation "Top Five, Bottom Ten"

TIME

1 hour and 10 minutes, which includes setup, the activity, and a debriefing

SUPPLIES AND RESOURCES

- Barriers and Bridges handout (number 8) for all participants
- The Thirty Leadership Behaviors handout (number 2) with Top Five, Bottom Ten identified from the LPI Action Card Shuffle (Activity 5), Variation "Top Five, Bottom Ten," or:
- LPI Survey Report, turned to the Leadership Behaviors Ranking page (if participants have completed the LPI)
- LPI Action Card deck for each participant
- 5-by-7-inch Post-it® Notes (one or two packages per group)
- Markers (one per person)

FACILITATOR NOTES

Activity Setup

- Divide participants into table groups of three to five. Explain that participants will work in small groups to identify barriers to demonstrating leadership behaviors. For this activity, each group will need access to large Post-it Notes and markers.

Overview

Even with the best intentions, focusing on developing our leadership can be derailed by day-to-day happenings. Whether it's "time" or "lack of support" or "lack of response," we often have difficulty maintaining a development focus. At times, leaders become discouraged when they try a new behavior and the response is not what they desired. In leadership, as in all skills that we develop, we need practice, practice, practice! So rather than giving up on a leadership behavior, leaders should develop ways to address the barriers that get in their way.

The purpose of this activity is to provide an opportunity for leaders to determine barriers to their leadership development and to create tactics that will help them address and overcome those barriers to leadership.

Introduce the Activity

1. Distribute the Barriers and Bridges handout to all participants.
2. Have each participant complete Part 1: Barriers to Leadership on the handout by sorting through their LPI Action Card decks to locate the behavior that he/she wants to improve. Participants can also refer to The Thirty Leadership Behaviors handout with Top Five, Bottom Ten Identified from the LPI Action Card Shuffle (Activity 5), Variation "Top Five, Bottom Ten," or their LPI Survey Report, turned to the Leadership Behaviors Ranking page (if participants have completed the LPI. Allow five to seven minutes.
3. Instruct participants to write their barriers on the Post-it Notes provided. They should write one barrier per note.
4. Instruct participants to pick the top three barriers that, if addressed, would have an impact on their ability to practice the leadership behavior they indicated for development. They should number them 1, 2, and 3 on the Post-its.
5. Next, ask participants to stand up and move to the wall, maintaining their groups. Post their notes on the wall, like building blocks, and then share, in turn, the leadership behavior and the barriers.
6. Once all group members have shared their barriers, they will focus on their top three barriers and seek advice and coaching from the other group members, writing the suggestions they receive on their Post-it Notes. Allow twenty to thirty minutes.
7. When the groups have completed their discussions, instruct them to take seats and complete Part 2: Bridges to Build

Leadership on their Barriers and Bridges handouts. Allow five to seven minutes.

Complete the Activity

Once participants have completed their handouts, have volunteers share with the group the behaviors they are focusing on, barriers they experience, and tactics they will use in the future. Encourage participants to think about the next time that they will experience the barrier and plan on how they will use the tactics they planned.

Debrief

Ask participants the following questions, and probe for more information when necessary:

- *What are some of the more common barriers that you heard in your groups?*
    (Possible responses: time, fear of trying something different, lack of positive response from direct reports)
- *What will you do if your tactic doesn't seem to work the first time?*
    (Possible responses: try again, as changed behavior comes with practice, so it requires more than one try)

Wrap Up

The purpose of this activity was to provide an opportunity for leaders to determine barriers to their leadership development and to create tactics that will help them address and overcome those barriers. Say that they should continue to focus on indentifying barriers to utilizing the leadership behaviors and developing tactics that address barriers to developing their leadership skills.

As Kouzes and Posner say, "Leaders are learners." To learn, continue to practice, practice, practice your leadership.

Thank the group for their participation.

VARIATIONS

1. **Role Play:** Practicing a behavior in the face of challenges and barriers is difficult. If leaders role play using the leadership behaviors, they gain practice in a controlled environment. Speaking the words he/she would use in a particular situation challenges a leader, prepares him or her to address the situation, and provides a great learning opportunity. To create a role play that applies to the leaders' barriers, follow the steps below.
   - Logistics:
     - The ideal number of participants per group is three. This allows each person to play the role of leader.
     - This will add approximately thirty minutes per leader or ninety minutes overall.
   - Have participants select who will go first, second, and third in leading their own role plays. As each role play begins, non-leaders will play the other characters in the scenario based on the instruction by the leader. For example, in role play 1, there will be a leader and participants playing two roles chosen by the leader (perhaps two direct reports or a colleague and an observer). If there are more participants than roles, ask the remaining people to observe and take notes.
   - Using the notes they have taken about which leadership behaviors they'd use and how, the leader will address the other characters regarding the issue. Allow approximately five minutes for the leaders to write a few bullet points for how they would approach the issue.

- Create the following flip chart to provide direction:

> 1. Get into groups of three people.
> 2. Choose leaders:
>   - Role Play 1 (Leader 1): _____
>   - Role Play 2 (Leader 2): _____
>   - Role Play 3 (Leader 3): _____
> 3. Leaders all spend five minutes; list bullet points on what you will say.
> 4. Role Play 1: What are the roles and who will play them? Observer?
> 5. Conduct the role play: ten minutes.
> 6. Give feedback: ten minutes.
> 7. Switch to next role play: switch leaders, characters

- Conduct the role play and allow time for feedback to the leaders about how well they used the appropriate leadership behaviors.
- Debrief by asking the following questions:
  - *What did you learn about using the leadership behaviors?*
  - *What was difficult about the role play?*
  - *What did you see as observers or other characters that was done effectively by the leaders?*
  - *As leaders, what did you think you could have done better?*
  - *How will what you have learned help you with the situation you addressed?*
  - *How will this role-play activity impact the way that you use the leadership behaviors in your daily work?*

2. **LPI Card Shuffle:** On a weekly or bi-weekly basis, leaders should shuffle the LPI Action Card decks and then select one behavior for focus for the given period (one or two weeks). Using a journal or planner, leaders develop ideas for improvement in

this behavior, the barriers they may face, and the tactics they **will** use to overcome the barriers. They should consider what they **are** doing well, what they can do better, and plan for their next opportunity to use this behavior. If they have completed the *Leadership Practices Inventory*, they should consider their LPI feedback (especially the page Ranking the Thirty Behaviors) when doing the activity.

COACH'S NOTES

If you are working one-on-one with a leader, you can adapt this activity. Have the leader complete Part 1 of the Barriers and Bridges handout in advance of your coaching session. Discuss the leadership behavior and barriers and develop an approach with the leader about how to address the barrier and what tactics might be most appropriate. If time permits, role play the situation with the leader. Come to agreement on a specific situation in which the leader will practice using the leadership behavior and the tactics and discuss the results in your next coaching session.

HANDOUT 8
BARRIERS AND BRIDGES

"The only way that people can learn is by doing things they've never done before."

—Jim Kouzes and Barry Posner

PART 1: BARRIERS TO LEADERSHIP

Which behavior would you like to improve:

Behavior # _____ Behavior _____

What is the benefit in improving this behavior?

_____

_____

_____

What are the barriers that you experience in trying to practice this behavior? (Examples could include "time," "lack of support by my leader," "poor response when tried the behavior," etc.)

_____

_____

_____

PART 2: BRIDGES TO BUILD LEADERSHIP

After discussing the barriers to leadership, what tactics did you define to help address your top three barriers?

Barrier 1: _____

Tactic: _____

_____

_____

Barrier 2: _____

Tactic: _____

_____

_____

Barrier 3: _____

Tactic: _____

_____

_____

HANDOUT 2
THE THIRTY LEADERSHIP BEHAVIORS

The Five Practices of Exemplary Leadership	The Thirty Leadership Behaviors
Model the Way	1. Sets a personal example of what he/she expects of others.
	6. Makes certain that people adhere to agreed-on standards.
	11. Follows through on promises and commitments.
	16. Asks for feedback for how his/her actions affect people's performance.
	21. Builds consensus around organization's values.
	26. Is clear about his/her philosophy of leadership.
Inspire a Shared Vision	2. Talks about future trends influencing our work.
	7. Describes a compelling image of the future.
	12. Appeals to others to share dream of the future.
	17. Shows others how their interests can be realized.
	22. Paints "big picture" of group aspirations.
	27. Speaks with conviction about the meaning of work.

Leadership Practices Inventory (LPI) Action Cards
Copyright © 2010 by James M. Kouzes and Barry Z. Posner.
Reproduced by permission of Pfeiffer, an Imprint of Wiley. www.pfeiffer.com.

The Five Practices of Exemplary Leadership	The Thirty Leadership Behaviors
Challenge the Process	3. Seeks challenging opportunities to test skills. 8. Challenges people to try new approaches. 13. Searches outside organization for innovative ways to improve. 18. Asks "What can we learn?" 23. Makes certain that goals, plans, and milestones are set. 28. Experiments and takes risks.
Enable Others to Act	4. Develops cooperative relationships. 9. Actively listens to diverse points of view. 14. Treats people with dignity and respect. 19. Supports decisions other people make. 24. Gives people choice about how to do their work. 29. Ensures that people grow in their jobs.
Encourage the Heart	5. Praises people for a job well done. 10. Expresses confidence in people's abilities. 15. Creatively rewards people for their contributions. 20. Recognizes people for commitment to shared values. 25. Finds ways to celebrate accomplishments. 30. Gives team members appreciation and support.

Leadership Practices Inventory (LPI) Action Cards
Copyright © 2010 by James M. Kouzes and Barry Z. Posner.
Reproduced by permission of Pfeiffer, an Imprint of Wiley. www.pfeiffer.com.

ACTIVITY 8
LEADERSHIP BEHAVIOR
COMBINATIONS

ACTIVITY OVERVIEW

This activity provides leaders with the opportunity to learn about how different leadership behaviors can be used in combination to strengthen their leadership.

PURPOSE

The purpose of this activity is to provide leaders with information on how leadership behaviors, when used in combination, can strengthen their leadership further. As a result of this activity, leaders will be able to:

- Identify the leadership behaviors that, when used in combination, create:
  - Credibility
  - Collaboration
  - Results-Orientation
- Use the leadership behaviors to strengthen their credibility, collaboration, and results-orientation.

PARTICIPANTS

Minimum: 3
Maximum: 30
Recommended: 12
(Participants work in groups of four or five during this activity.)

PREREQUISITE

Familiarity with LPI behaviors. Suggested pre-work includes introductory activities such as the LPI Action Card Leadership Case Studies (Activity 3) as well as completion of the *Leadership Practices Inventory.*

TIME

1 hour, which includes setup, the activity, and a debriefing

SUPPLIES AND RESOURCES

- Leadership Behavior Combinations handout (number 9)
- LPI Action Card deck for each participant
- Three flip-chart stands, paper, and markers

FACILITATOR NOTES

Activity Setup

- For groups of fifteen or fewer, set up three flip-chart stands with flip-chart paper. If your group is larger, you will want to have three additional stands, or at least have flip-chart paper available.

Overview

The purpose of this activity is to provide leaders with information on how leadership behaviors, when used in combination, can strengthen their leadership further. As a result of this activity, leaders will be able to identify the leadership behaviors that, when used in combination, create credibility, collaboration, and results-orientation. Leaders can then use the appropriate leadership behaviors to strengthen these areas of their leadership.

Introduce the Activity

1. Distribute the Leadership Behavior Combinations handout.
2. Share information on credibility: *As Kouzes and Posner say, "Credibility is the foundation of leadership." Research has found that trustworthiness, expertise, and dynamism are the building blocks of credibility. This is very similar to research by Kouzes and Posner that found that "honest," "competent," and "inspiring" are three characteristics that are essential to leadership.*
3. Share the three behaviors that make up credibility: numbers 14, 11, and 1. Ask participants to note these on their handouts. They are

    14. Treats people with dignity and respect
    11. Follows through on promises and commitments
    1. Sets a personal example of what he/she expects of others
    Ask: *Why do you think these are so important for credibility?*
4. Share information on collaboration: *Leadership is about relationships. Building collaboration is at the heart of building strong relationships. Two key factors in collaboration are trust and facilitation of relationships. Leaders trust first, as Kouzes and Posner say, and they involve others in getting things done.*
5. Share the four behaviors that make up collaboration: 4, 9, 14, and 24. Ask participants to note these on their handouts. They are

    4. Develops cooperative relationships
    9. Actively listens to diverse points of view
    14. Treats people with dignity and respect
    24. Gives people choice about how to do their work
    Ask: *Why do you think these are so important for collaboration?*
6. Share information on results-orientation. The five behaviors that make up results-orientation are 23, 6, 1, 11, and 8. Ask participants to note these on their handouts. They are

    23. Makes certain that goals, plans, and milestones are set

6. Makes certain that people adhere to agreed-upon standards

1. Sets a personal example of what he/she expects of others

11. Follows through on promises and commitments

8. Challenges people to try new approaches

Ask: *Why do you think these are so important for getting results?*

7. Set up the brainstorming activity. Create three groups of three to five people each. Each group will focus on one of the leadership behavior combinations. They will brainstorm specific actions they can take to improve their leadership on the assigned combination and write these actions on flip-chart pages. These could be specific to the behaviors or ideas for the combination in general. (Note: if you have a group larger than fifteen, assign one or two groups to each combination.)

Complete the Activity

When the groups have finished, have them walk around the room to see the ideas for each of the leadership behavior combinations. Participants can jot down notes of ideas that they like. When they return to their desks, ask them to complete Part 2: Applying Leadership Behavior Combinations on the handout.

Debrief

Ask participants the following questions, and probe for more information when necessary:

- *What are some of the ideas or actions that you plan on applying for Credibility?*
- *How about Collaboration?*
- *And Results-Orientation?*

Wrap Up

The purpose of this activity was to provide leaders with information on how leadership behaviors, when used in combination, can strengthen their leadership further. Leaders can now use the leadership behaviors to strengthen these areas of their leadership.

Encourage participants to practice the actions they committed to as soon as possible.

Thank the group for their participation.

VARIATIONS

1. **Build the Combinations:** To create a lively discussion and test leaders' knowledge of the behaviors, have small groups guess which leadership behaviors make up Credibility, Collaboration, and Results-Orientation prior to the brainstorming activity. Using one deck of LPI Action Cards per group of three or four participants, have them sort through the cards to determine the three behaviors that make up Credibility. Have teams shout out when they think they have an answer, and allow challenges by other groups. Do this for each leadership behavior combination and then provide the answers for them to write on their handouts.

COACH'S NOTES

If you are working one-on-one with a leader, you can adapt this activity. Work together with the leader to complete Part 1 of the Leadership Behavior Combinations handout during your coaching session. Discuss the leader's scores or assessment of these leadership behaviors and develop an approach to address the person's development in each of these. Come to agreement on a specific situation in which the leader will practice using the leadership behavior combinations and discuss the results with you in his/her next coaching session.

HANDOUT 9
LEADERSHIP BEHAVIOR COMBINATIONS

*"Credibility is the foundation
of leadership."*
—Jim Kouzes and Barry Posner

PART 1: LEADERSHIP BEHAVIOR COMBINATIONS

1. Which three behaviors make up Credibility?

   Behavior # _____ Behavior _____

   Behavior # _____ Behavior _____

   Behavior # _____ Behavior _____

2. Which four behaviors make up Collaboration?

   Behavior # _____ Behavior _____

   Behavior # _____ Behavior _____

   Behavior # _____ Behavior _____

   Behavior # _____ Behavior _____

3. Which five behaviors make up Results-Orientation?

Behavior # _____ Behavior _____

Behavior # _____ Behavior _____

Behavior # _____ Behavior _____

Behavior # _____ Behavior _____

Behavior # _____ Behavior _____

PART 2: APPLYING LEADERSHIP BEHAVIOR COMBINATIONS

After brainstorming ways to improve Credibility, Collaboration, and Results-Orientation, list actions that you will take here.

Credibility:

_____

_____

_____

_____

_____

_____

_____

_____

Collaboration:

_____

_____

_____

_____

_____

_____

_____

_____

_____

_____

Results-Orientation:

_____

_____

_____

_____

_____

_____

_____

_____

_____

ACTIVITY 9
FEEDBACK AND COACHING CIRCLE

ACTIVITY OVERVIEW

In this activity, leaders work in small groups to obtain feedback on the LPI leadership behaviors from others they work with regularly.

PURPOSE

The purpose of this activity is to provide leaders with the opportunity to hear feedback on how they are utilizing the LPI leadership behaviors. As a result of this activity, leaders will be able to:

- Improve on LPI Behavior 16, "Asks for feedback on how his/her actions affect people's performance."
- Receive and act on feedback regarding their strengths and developmental areas.
- Provide feedback and coaching to others regarding their leadership.

PARTICIPANTS

Minimum: 2
Maximum: 30
Recommended: 12 to 15
(Participants work on their own or in groups of three for this activity.)

PREREQUISITE

In this activity, participants must work with each other frequently enough to be able to provide meaningful feedback. Familiarity with LPI behaviors is required. Suggested pre-work includes introductory activities such as "Leaders Tell Us..." and the Leadership Behaviors Board Game, as well as completion of the *Leadership Practices Inventory*.

TIME

1 hour and 50 minutes, including setup, the activity, and debriefing

SUPPLIES AND RESOURCES

- LPI Action Card deck for each group
- LPI Survey Report, turned to the Leadership Behaviors Ranking page (if participants have completed the LPI)
- Feedback and Coaching Circle handout (number 10)

FACILITATOR NOTES

Activity Setup
- For this activity, divide participants into pairs or groups of three.
- Distribute the Feedback and Coaching Circle handout to all participants.
- Distribute one deck of LPI Action Cards per table.

Overview
The purpose of this activity is to provide leaders with the opportunity to obtain feedback on how they are utilizing

the LPI leadership behaviors. As a result of this activity, leaders will be able to improve on LPI Behavior 16, "Asks for feedback on how his/her actions affect people's performance." They will also receive and act on feedback regarding their strengths and developmental areas and provide feedback and coaching to others regarding their leadership.

In Kouzes and Posner's most recent analysis of LPI data, taken from 70,000 leaders[*] who have taken the LPI, they found that the behavior that is consistently at the bottom of the ranking of thirty behaviors is number 16, "Asks for feedback on how his/her actions affect the performance of others."[*]

Providing structured process allows leaders to practice asking for feedback.

Introduce the Activity

1. Form groups of two or three, ensuring that the participants in each group are familiar enough with one another to provide feedback on others' leadership behaviors.
2. Choose which leader will go first, second, and third in receiving feedback.
3. Leader 1 selects one behavior from the deck of LPI Action Cards that he/she would like **to improve** and one behavior that he/she sees as a **strength**. The leader places these cards on the table for the other participants to see. (Leaders can refer to the LPI Survey Report, turned to the Leadership Behaviors Ranking page to help them select behaviors if they have completed the *Leadership Practices Inventory*.)

---

*James M. Kouzes and Barry Z. Posner, The Leadership Challenge *(4th ed.). San Francisco: Jossey-Bass, 2007.*

4. The participants providing feedback now complete Section 1 on the Feedback and Coaching Circle handout for Leader 1. Provide seven to ten minutes for this portion of the activity. The questions include:
   - What is the behavior name and number of a strength of this leader?
   - List a workplace example of when this leader has done this behavior well. (What did the leader do or say to demonstrate this behavior? Who was involved?)
   - What was the impact or result of the action that the leader took?
   - What could the leader do to continue to leverage this strength?
   - What is the name and number of a behavior for development for this leader?
   - List a workplace example of when this leader has done this behavior well. (What did the leader do or say to demonstrate this behavior? Who was involved?)
   - What was the impact or result of the action that the leader took?
   - List a workplace example of when this leader could have done this behavior better. (What did the leader do or say? Who was involved?)
   - What was the impact or result of the action that the leader took?
   - What would be the impact of the revised actions?

   Now practice LPI Behavior 10, "Expresses confidence in people's abilities."
   - What can you say that expresses your confidence in this leader?

5. Once all observer/coaches have completed the "Observer/ Coach" sections for Leader 1, they take turns providing feedback. Provide these instructions:

- *Share your feedback with the leader and allow him/her to ask questions about the situation. Add additional coaching and feedback to the leader throughout your conversation as needed.*

- *Take approximately seven to ten minutes per observer to provide feedback.*

6. After each observer has provided feedback, allow the leader to complete Section 3 on the handout. Allow five to seven minutes for this part of the activity. The reflection questions include:

- What is the behavior name and number of one of your leadership strengths?

- Jot down your thoughts regarding the situations mentioned by the observers for when you've done this behavior well.

- What ideas did you hear from the observers to help you continue to leverage this strength?

- What is the name and number of your leadership behavior targeted for development?

- Jot down your thoughts and ideas regarding the situations mentioned by observers for when you may have done this behavior better.

- What actions will you take to demonstrate this behavior in the future?

Complete the Activity

Switch to the next leader and repeat until each leader has received feedback.

Debrief

Ask participants the following questions, and probe for more information when necessary:

- Sharing your feedback with others can be especially helpful to others if they are working on the same or similar behaviors. What leadership behavior were you focused on developing as a leader?
- What were some of the strengths that you were focused on leveraging?
- What feedback did you receive that was particularly helpful to you?

Wrap Up

The purpose of this activity was to provide leaders with the opportunity to receive feedback on how they are utilizing the LPI leadership behaviors. *Say: You now have a great way to improve on LPI Behavior 16, "Asks for feedback on how his/her actions affect people's performance." To develop your leadership, you must first develop yourself. Feedback is the perfect avenue to understand where you need to grow as a leader. As Kouzes and Posner put it:*

> *The instrument of leadership is the self, and the mastery of the art of leadership comes from the mastery of the self.*
>
> *James M. Kouzes and Barry Z. Posner,* The Leadership Challenge *(4th ed.). San Francisco: Jossey-Bass, 2007.*

Encourage participants to continue to seek feedback and thank the group for their participation.

VARIATIONS

1. **Feedback Roundtable:** This variation provides a quick opportunity for leaders to receive feedback on a single behavior in a team meeting. To conduct this variation, follow the steps below.
   - Set aside enough time in a meeting so that the leader can receive feedback from those attending the meeting. (If this is a large group, it may take quite a while. Not everyone in the meeting may have feedback, so do not press people to provide it.)
   - The leader selects a card from the deck showing a behavior on which he/she would like to receive feedback and shares some context on why he/she would like to improve this behavior. The behavior may include behaviors that are lower in his/her LPI results (or in his/her own assessment of his/her behaviors, or it may be a card that he/she is focusing on for the week/month (see the LPI Action Card Shuffle, Activity 5).
   - Others in the meeting jot down specific examples of when the leader has done this well or when he/she could have improved, and what the person could do differently.
   - Those who have examples share ways that the leader could improve, then share what the leader is doing well.
   - The leader may ask questions to clarify or to receive further ideas for development.

2. **One-on-One with the Thirty Behaviors:** This variation is suggested for pairs. It is more thorough feedback because it allows observers to review all thirty behaviors and share feedback on a few of the top and bottom behaviors.
   - The person providing feedback (observer) sorts through the thirty behavior cards, a subset that the leader selects, or just a few of the cards that the leader would like feedback on. If starting with the full deck or a large subset of the cards

(say, top five and bottom ten behaviors), the observer quickly sorts the cards into three piles according to how frequently he or she witnesses the behavior:

- Frequently
- Sometimes
- Not Often
- The observer then selects one or two cards and provides feedback to the leader using Section 1 on the Feedback and Coaching Circle handout.
- The observer may also want to provide feedback on why each card is in the pile in which it is located. This takes considerable time, but would provide great insight, especially if provided by the leader's supervisor or close peer.

COACH'S NOTES

If you are working one-on-one with a leader, you can adapt this activity. If you are familiar enough with the leader's day-to-day behaviors, you could complete the Feedback and Coaching Circle handout and provide feedback or else complete Variation 2 above. If you are not able to observe the daily behaviors of the leader, you might suggest that he or she work with a close colleague or supervisor to complete Variation 2 above, and share with you the cards that fell into each category. You can then coach the leader around the behaviors he/she most wants to improve. Then discuss the person's answers and work with him/her to develop the actions he/she will take.

HANDOUT 10
FEEDBACK AND
COACHING CIRCLE

SECTION 1: OBSERVER/COACH FOR LEADER 1

Leader's Strength:

- What is the behavior name and number of one of this leader's strengths?

  Behavior Number: _____   Behavior Name: _____

- List a workplace example of when this leader has done this behavior well. (What did the leader do or say to demonstrate this behavior? Who was involved?)

- What was the impact or result of the action that the leader took?

- What could the leader do to continue to leverage this strength?

Leader's Behavior for Development:

- What is the name and number of a behavior for development for this leader?

  Behavior Number: _____   Behavior Name: _____

- List a workplace example of when this leader has done this behavior well. (What did the leader do or say to demonstrate this behavior? Who was involved?)

- What was the impact or result of the action that the leader took?

- List a workplace example of when this leader could have done this behavior better. (What did the leader do or say? Who was involved?)

- What was the impact or result of the action that the leader took?

- What would be the impact of the revised actions?

Practice LPI Behavior 10, "Expresses confidence in people's abilities."

- What can you say that expresses your confidence in this leader?

SECTION 2: OBSERVER/COACH FOR LEADER 2

Leader's Strength:

- What is the behavior name and number of one of this leader's strengths?

  Behavior Number: _____ Behavior Name: _____

- List a workplace example of when this leader has done this behavior well. (What did the leader do or say to demonstrate this behavior? Who was involved?)

- What was the impact or result of the action that the leader took?

- What could the leader do to continue to leverage this strength?

Leader's Behavior for Development:

- What is the name and number of a behavior for development for this leader?

  Behavior Number: _____   Behavior name: _____

- List a workplace example of when this leader has done this behavior well. (What did the leader do or say to demonstrate this behavior? Who was involved?)

- What was the impact or result of the action that the leader took?

- List a workplace example of when this leader could have done this behavior better. (What did the leader do or say? Who was involved?)

Leadership Practices Inventory (LPI) Action Cards
Copyright © 2010 by James M. Kouzes and Barry Z. Posner.
Reproduced by permission of Pfeiffer, an Imprint of Wiley. www.pfeiffer.com.

- What was the impact or result of the action that the leader took?

- What would be the impact of the revised actions?

Practice LPI Behavior 10, "Expresses confidence in people's abilities."

- What can you say that expresses your confidence in this leader?

SECTION 3: LEADER NOTES

Leadership Strength:

- What is the behavior name and number of one of your leadership strengths?

  Behavior Number: _____   Behavior Name: _____

- Jot down your thoughts regarding the situations mentioned by the observers for when you've done this behavior well.

- What ideas did you hear from the observers to help you continue to leverage this strength?

Leadership Behavior for Development:

- What is the name and number of your leadership behavior targeted for development?

  Behavior Number: _____   Behavior Name: _____

- Jot down your thoughts and ideas regarding the situations mentioned by observers for when you may have done this behavior better.

- What actions will you take to demonstrate this behavior in the future?

Observer 1:

_____

_____

_____

_____

_____

Observer 2:

_____

_____

_____

_____

_____

_____

_____

_____